Practical MATH

AGS

by
Wilmer L. Jones, Ph.D.

AGS®

American Guidance Service, Inc.
4201 Woodland Road
Circle Pines, MN 55014-1796
1-800-328-2560

Life Skills Mathematics

Printed in the United States of America

ISBN 0–7854–0952–1 (Previously ISBN 0–88671–555–5)

Product Number 90860

A 0 9 8 7 6 5 4 5 3

Contents

Unit 1: Banking Services

Skill Building: Addition and Subtraction of Decimals   5
Lesson 1: Savings Accounts   6
Lesson 2: Compound Interest, Part 1   8
Lesson 3: Compound Interest, Part 2   10
Lesson 4: Deposits and Withdrawals   12
Lesson 5: Checking Accounts   14
Skill Building: Multiplying by 10, 100, and 1,000   17
Lesson 6: Check Registers   18
Skill Building: Rounding Decimals   20
Skill Building: Percents to Decimals,
     Decimals to Percents   21

Unit 2: Budgeting Income

Lesson 1: Hourly Pay and Overtime   22
Lesson 2: Commissions   24
Lesson 3: Gross and Net Pay   26
Lesson 4: Budget Record   28
Lesson 5: Preparing a Budget   32
Lesson 6: Preparing a Budget Record Sheet   34
Skill Building: Multiplication of Decimals   36

Unit 3: Consumer Credit

Lesson 1: Credit Card Purchasing   38
Lesson 2: Installment Purchasing   40
Lesson 3: Short-Term Loans   42
Lesson 4: Cost of Credit   44
Skill Building: Finding a Percent of a Number   46
Skill Building: Dividing a Decimal by a Whole Number   47
Mid-Book Test: Units 1–3   48

Unit 4: Purchasing a Car

Lesson 1: Cost of a New or Used Car   50
Lesson 2: Financing a Car   52
Lesson 3: Maintenance Costs   54
Lesson 4: Auto Insurance   56
Skill Building: Dividing a Decimal by a Decimal   58

Unit 5: Purchasing a House

Lesson 1: Mortgage Loans 60

Lesson 2: Monthly Mortgage Payments 62

Lesson 3: Real Estate Tax 64

Lesson 4: Homeowners Insurance 66

Skill Building: Finding What Percent One
Number Is of Another 68

Skill Building: Writing Fractions in Lowest Terms 69

Unit 6: Taxes

Lesson 1: Sales Tax 70

Lesson 2: Social Security 72

Lesson 3: Adjusted Gross Income 74

Lesson 4: Taxable Income 76

Lesson 5: State Income Tax 78

Skill Building: Addition and Subtraction of Fractions 80

Unit 7: Investments

Lesson 1: Certificates of Deposit 82

Lesson 2: Buying and Selling Stock 84

Skill Building: Writing Fractions as Percents 87

Lesson 3: Bonds 88

Lesson 4: Savings Bonds 90

Lesson 5: Rate of Return 92

End-of-Book Test 95

Addition and Subtraction of Decimals

Rules to Remember:

To add and subtract decimals:

➤ Line up the decimal points in the addends under each other.

➤ Annex (insert) zeros where necessary.

➤ Add or subtract as with whole numbers.

Examples:

Add: 12.75 + 4.085 + 16

```
    12.750   Annex zero
     4.085
  + 16.000   Annex zeros
    32.835
```
  ↑ Decimal point under other decimal points

Subtract: 275.5 – 98.653

```
   275.500   Annex zeros
  – 98.653
   176.847
```
  ↑ Decimal point under other decimal points

A Add to find the sum.

1. 27.5 + 18.23 + 6.28 = _____

2. 27.4 + 19.86 + 8 = _____

3. 276.3 + 198.27 + 48 = _____

4. .072 + .18 + 1.4 = _____

5. 57.45 + .0745 + 4.5 = _____

6. 33 + .03 + 3.343 = _____

7. 9.546 + .04 + 4.96 = _____

8. 342 + 23.42 + .23 = _____

9. 71.15 + 711.51 + .515 = _____

10. .08 + 80.88 + 8.898 = _____

B Subtract to find the difference.

11. 2.75 – 1.682 = _____

12. 38.24 – 12.921 = _____

13. 18 – 6.25 = _____

14. 2.0756 – 1.176 = _____

15. 42.65 – 32.601 = _____

16. 93 – 62.95 = _____

17. 6.51 – 3.5324 = _____

18. 10.975 – 9.05 = _____

19. 45.817 – 32 = _____

20. 288 – 287.089 = _____

Savings Accounts

Banks offer many services for consumers. For example, banks provide a safe place for people to invest their money. These investments earn money for the customer and for the bank. When money is deposited in a savings account, it earns *interest*. The *principal* is the money that is deposited in the account that is earning interest. The *annual interest rate* is the percent of interest paid in one year on the principal. *Simple interest* is interest paid only on the original principal.

Example: James Robinson has $2,000 deposited in a savings account with an annual interest rate of 8%. How much interest did he earn in 9 months?

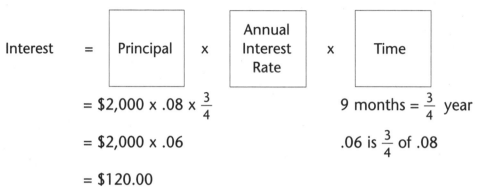

Interest = | Principal | x | Annual Interest Rate | x | Time |

$$= \$2,000 \times .08 \times \frac{3}{4} \qquad 9 \text{ months} = \frac{3}{4} \text{ year}$$

$$= \$2,000 \times .06 \qquad .06 \text{ is } \frac{3}{4} \text{ of } .08$$

$$= \$120.00$$

The interest earned in 9 months was $120.00.

A Find the interest earned.

1. Fred Czarnec
   $5,000 deposited
   7% annual interest rate
   Time: 1 year

   _____

2. Steve Haar
   $4,500 deposited
   6% annual interest rate
   Time: 6 months

   _____

3. Carol Jones
   $500 deposited
   $7\frac{1}{2}$% annual interest rate
   Time: 2 years

   _____

4. Toni Thompson
   $2,400 deposited
   $6\frac{1}{2}$% annual interest rate
   Time: 9 months

   _____

B Find the simple interest on each deposit.

	Person	Principal	Annual Rate	Time	Interest
5.	Tom Stills	$800	$5\frac{1}{2}$%	1 year	
6.	Erin Lavie	2,000	8%	6 months	
7.	Carlos Fernandez	150	$7\frac{1}{2}$%	2 years	
8.	Tyrone Willis	4,000	8%	9 months	
9.	Mary Jones	750	6.5%	3 years	
10.	Chris Yetman	6,000	6%	$2\frac{1}{2}$ years	
11.	Rashid Mustaf	1,500	12%	3 months	
12.	Alice Green	4,200	9%	18 months	
13.	Thomas Foster	7,500	$5\frac{1}{2}$%	6 years	
14.	Amy Ling	900	4%	$1\frac{3}{4}$ years	
15.	Karen Menshaw	8,000	8%	6 months	

16. On April 1, Alice Brown deposited $4,000 in her savings account. It paid an annual interest rate of $6\frac{1}{2}$%. How much simple interest has she earned by October? _____

17. John Savarese deposited $2,500 in his savings account. It paid an 8% annual interest rate. How much simple interest did he earn after a year and a half? _____

Compound Interest, Part 1

After interest is earned, it is added to the savings account. When the new balance is used as the principal for the next interest period, you are receiving *compound interest.* Compound interest is the interest earned on the original principal as well as on all the interest earned during the previous interest period.

Example: June Gary has $1,000 deposited in a savings account paying an annual interest rate of 6%. The interest on the account is compounded yearly. What is the amount in her account after the second year?

| Annual Interest | = | Principal | × | Interest Rate | × | Time |

$$= \$1,000 \times .06 \times 1$$
$$= \$60.00$$

After the first year, the new principal is $1,000 + $60.00 interest, or $1,060.

| Annual Interest | = | Principal | × | Interest Rate | × | Time |

$$= \$1,060 \times .06 \times 1$$
$$= \$63.60$$

After the second year, the amount in her account is $1,060 + $63.60 interest, or $1,123.60.

A Find the amount in each account after three years. The interest is compounded yearly.

	1.	2.	3.	4.	5.	6.	7.
Principal	$2,000	$500	$4,000	$1,500	$2,500	$3,000	$10,000
Annual Interest Rate	5%	8%	6%	8%	9%	7%	$7\frac{1}{2}$%
First Interest							
Amount after 1 Yr.							
Second Interest							
Amount after 2 Yr.							
Third Interest							
Amount after 3 Yr.							

B Find the amount in each account. The interest is compounded yearly.

8. José Sanchez
Principal: $1,500
Annual interest rate: 6%
Amount after 2 years?

_____

9. Alice Morgan-Brown
Principal: $4,000
Annual interest rate: $6\frac{1}{2}$%
Amount after 3 years?

_____

10. Paul Budny
Principal: $800
Annual interest rate: 7%
Amount after 4 years?

_____

11. William Moulds
Principal: $6,500
Annual interest rate: 8%
Amount after 5 years?

_____

12. Maria Santos
Principal: $1,800
Annual interest rate: 4%
Amount after 3 years?

_____

13. Bradley Johnson
Principal: $3,000
Annual interest rate: $5\frac{1}{2}$%
Amount after 4 years?

_____

14. Sarah Cohen
Principal: $5,125
Annual interest rate: 6%
Amount after 4 years?

_____

15. Lisa Wong
Principal: $2,400
Annual interest rate: $6\frac{1}{2}$%
Amount after 5 years?

_____

16. On June 1, Daniel Cox deposited $1,200 in a savings account paying 8% interest compounded yearly. Four years later he withdrew the full amount. How much was this? _____

Compound Interest, Part 2

Tables such as the one below are often used to compute the amount of compound interest more quickly. The *compound interest table* shows how much $1 will amount to after a given number of years at various rates of interest compounded annually.

						GROWTH OF ONE DOLLAR AT INTEREST COMPOUNDED ANNUALLY					
n	$1\frac{1}{2}\%$	2%	$2\frac{1}{2}\%$	3%	$3\frac{1}{2}\%$	4%	5%	6%	7%	8%
1	1.0150	1.0200	1.0250	1.0300	1.0350	1.0400	1.0500	1.0600	1.0700	1.0800
2	1.0302	1.0404	1.0506	1.0609	1.0712	1.0816	1.1025	1.1236	1.1449	1.1664
3	1.0457	1.0612	1.0769	1.0927	1.1087	1.1249	1.1576	1.1910	1.2250	1.2957
4	1.0614	1.0824	1.1038	1.1255	1.1475	1.1699	1.2155	1.2625	1.3108	1.3605
5	1.0773	1.1041	1.1314	1.1593	1.1877	1.2167	1.2763	1.3382	1.4026	1.4693
6	1.0934	1.1262	1.1597	1.1941	1.2293	1.2653	1.3401	1.4185	1.5007	1.5869
7	1.1098	1.1487	1.1887	1.2299	1.2723	1.3159	1.4071	1.5036	1.6058	1.7138
8	1.1265	1.1717	1.2184	1.2668	1.3168	1.3686	1.4775	1.5938	1.7182	1.8509
9	1.1434	1.1951	1.2489	1.3048	1.3629	1.4233	1.5513	1.6895	1.8385	1.9990
10	1.1605	1.2190	1.2801	1.3439	1.4106	1.4802	1.6289	1.7908	1.9672	2.1589
11	1.1779	1.2434	1.3121	1.3842	1.4600	1.5395	1.7103	1.8983	2.1049	2.3316
12	1.1956	1.2682	1.3449	1.4258	1.5111	1.6010	1.7959	2.0122	2.2522	2.5182
13	1.2136	1.2936	1.3785	1.4685	1.5640	1.6651	1.8856	2.1329	2.4098	2.7196
14	1.2318	1.3195	1.4130	1.5126	1.6187	1.7317	1.9799	2.2609	2.5785	2.9372
15	1.2502	1.3459	1.4483	1.5580	1.6753	1.8009	2.0789	2.3966	2.7590	3.1722
16	1.2690	1.3728	1.4845	1.6047	1.7340	1.8730	2.1829	2.5404	2.9522	3.4259
17	1.2880	1.4002	1.5216	1.6528	1.7947	1.9479	2.2920	2.6928	3.1588	3.7000
18	1.3073	1.4282	1.5597	1.7024	1.8575	2.0258	2.4066	2.8543	3.3799	3.9960
19	1.3270	1.4568	1.5987	1.7535	1.9225	2.1068	2.5270	3.0256	3.6165	4.3157
20	(1.3469)	1.4859	1.6386	1.8061	1.9898	2.1911	2.6533	3.2071	3.8697	4.6610

Value of $1 compounded annually for 20 years at $1\frac{1}{2}\%$ interest.

Example: Christa Jones had $3,500 deposited at $1\frac{1}{2}\%$ interest compounded annually. What is the amount in her account after 20 years?

In 20 years, $1 will amount to $1.3469 at $1\frac{1}{2}\%$ compounded annually.

Amount	=	Number of $1 in principal	x	Amount of $1 after 20 years

= 3,500 x $1.3469
= $4,714.15

The amount in her account after 20 years is $4,714.15.

A Use the compound interest table to find the value of $1 for the given interest rate and period of time.

1. Interest rate: 6%
   Time: 4 years _____

2. Interest rate: 8%
   Time: 10 years _____

3. Interest rate: 7%
   Time: 7 years _____

4. Interest rate: 6%
   Time: 20 years _____

5. Interest rate: 3%
   Time: 12 years _____

6. Interest rate: 5%
   Time: 8 years _____

B Find the amount in each account after the given period of time.

	Principal	Annual Rate	Time	Value of $1	Amount
7.	$2,000	$3\frac{1}{2}\%$	4 years		
8.	500	6%	5 years		
9.	1,500	7%	3 years		
10.	4,000	5%	8 years		
11.	800	8%	6 years		
12.	7,500	5%	9 years		
13.	1,200	6%	10 years		
14.	6,000	$2\frac{1}{2}\%$	12 years		
15.	650	8%	9 years		
16.	10,000	6%	12 years		
17.	3,000	4%	7 years		

18. At 6%, in about how many years would you be able to double your money? (See problem 16.) _____

19. At 8%, in about how many years would you be able to double your money? (See problem 15.) _____

20. At 4%, in about how many years would you be able to double your money? (Use the table on page 10.) _____

Deposits and Withdrawals

Banks usually issue *passbooks* so that you can keep a record of your savings account. When you make a deposit or a withdrawal, a bank teller records the transaction in the passbook. At certain times throughout the year, interest is recorded in the passbook.

Example: Laurie Wang has a savings account. On June 2 she deposited $250. The bank teller recorded the deposit and interest for the last year. What is the new balance in her passbook?

PASSBOOK ACCT. NO. 7123865				Laurie Wang
Date	**Interest**	**Deposit**	**Withdrawal**	**Balance**
Jan 8		$100.00		$185.00
March 15		150.00		335.00
June 2	$18.00	250.00		603.00
Sept 6	↑	↑	$75.00	↖

Interest   Deposit

Withdrawal

New Balance

1. How much did Laurie withdraw from her account on September 6? _____

2. What was the new balance after her withdrawal? _____

A Find the new balance.

	3.	4.	5.	6.	7.
Previous Balance	$275.90	$1,295.15	$816.75	$2,975.18	$1,603.12
Interest		60.20	15.75	150.75	42.50
Deposit	85.15	250.00		200.00	72.98
Withdrawal	125.00		150.00		175.00
New Balance					

8. On August 3, Betty Jaison made a deposit of $225.00. What is the new balance?

_____

PASSBOOK ACCT. NO. 1356428				Betty Jaison
Date	**Interest**	**Deposit**	**Withdrawal**	**Balance**
7/2		$150.00		$825.00
7/20	$15.50			840.50
8/3		225.00		

9. On April 2, Tom Seivers deposited $85.20 in his savings account. The teller also credited interest of $55.15 to his account. What is the new balance in his account?

PASSBOOK ACCT. NO. 3670334				Tom Seivers
Date	**Interest**	**Deposit**	**Withdrawal**	**Balance**
2/18		$100.00		$975.20
3/5		200.00		1,175.20
4/2	$55.15	85.20		

_____

B Find the balance for each date on each savings account.

PASSBOOK ACCT. NO. 2434827				
Date	**Interest**	**Deposit**	**Withdrawal**	**Balance**
7/19		$100.00		$925.80
8/1	$11.73			**10.**
8/20		195.20		**11.**
9/20		115.00		**12.**
11/2			$75.00	**13.**
12/1	13.21	165.00		**14.**

PASSBOOK ACCT. NO. 2256969				
Date	**Interest**	**Deposit**	**Withdrawal**	**Balance**
6/18		$80.55		$1,088.72
7/5	$12.34			**15.**
7/22			$125.00	**16.**
8/20		157.00		**17.**
10/5		92.61		**18.**
11/3	14.12	185.44		**19.**
11/8		122.93		**20.**

Checking Accounts

Another important service of banks is *checking accounts.* After a checking account is opened and a deposit is made, checks can be written against the account. The person who receives the check (*payee*) takes it to a bank for payment. The bank subtracts the amount of the check from the account of the person writing the check (*payer*). This is what a completed check looks like:

Example:

①

Tom Martin
2329 Main Street
West Valley, IN 47331
(717) 357-5555

②

300

June 2 19 *96*

PAY TO THE
ORDER OF *Speedy Muffler* $ *85.00*

③

Eighty-five and no/100 ——————————— DOLLARS

④

West Valley Springs
FOR *new muffler*   *Tom Martin*

‖ ■ 0 0333 2 ‖ ■ ■ ■ 0 5 2 0 0 0 6 1 8 ■   6 2 6 59 3 6 ‖ ■

⑤   ⑥

Things to Do:

To write a check, do the following:

1. Write the date.

2. Write the name of the person or business to whom the payment is made (payee).

3. Write the amount of the check in numerals.

4. Write the amount of the check in words.

5. Write a note on the check to show its purpose.

6. Sign the check (payer).

A Use the information above the check to complete it.

1.

Date	Payee	Amt. of check	For	Payer
12/20	Civil War Times	$18.95	Subscription	Wilmer Jones

WILMER JONES   205

_____19 _____

PAY TO THE
ORDER OF _____ $ _____

_____ DOLLARS

West Valley Springs

FOR _____   _____

‖■ 0 0333 2 ‖■ ■■ 0 5 2 0 0 0 6 1 8 ■   6 2 6 59 3 6 ‖■

B Use the information above the check to complete it.

2.

Date	Payee	Amt. of check	For	Payer
12/20	Mary's Dress Shop	$75.00	Dress	Mary Jane Harris

MARY JANE HARRIS   127

_____19 _____

PAY TO THE
ORDER OF _____ $ _____

_____ DOLLARS

West Valley Springs

FOR _____   _____

‖■ 0 0333 2 ‖■ ■■ 0 5 2 0 0 0 6 1 8 ■   6 2 6 59 3 6 ‖■

C Use the information above the check to complete it.

3.

Date	Payee	Amt. of check	For	Payer
6/12	Fast Food Store	$27.95	Groceries	Christa Woods

CHRISTA WOODS   615

_____ 19 _____

PAY TO THE
ORDER OF _____ $ _____

_____ DOLLARS

West Valley Springs

FOR _____ _____

⑂■ 0 0333 2 ⑂ ■ ■■ 0 5 2 0 0 0 6 1 8 ■   6 2 6 5 9 3 6 ⑂ ■

D Use the information above the check to complete it.

4.

Date	Payee	Amt. of check	For	Payer
7/25	Green Machine	$85.50	Lawn Care	Jim Cansey

JIM CANSEY   427

_____ 19 _____

PAY TO THE
ORDER OF _____ $ _____

_____ DOLLARS

West Valley Springs

FOR _____ _____

⑂■ 0 0333 2 ⑂ ■ ■■ 0 5 2 0 0 0 6 1 8 ■   6 2 6 5 9 3 6 ⑂ ■

Multiplying by 10, 100, and 1,000

Rules to Remember:

To multiply by 10, 100, or 1,000, move the decimal point to the right.

➤ To multiply by 10, move the decimal point *one* place to the right; by 100, *two* places to the right; by 1,000, *three* places to the right.

➤ When necessary, annex (insert) zeros to have the correct number of decimal places.

Examples:

Multiply 4.75 x 10   4.75 x 10 = 47.5

Multiply 7.3 x 1,000   7.3 x 1,000 = 7300   **Annex two zeros.**

 Multiply by 10.

1. 6.8

2. 13.72

3. .189

4. 69

5. .073

_____ _____ _____ _____ _____

B Multiply by 100.

6. 9.35

7. 8.072

8. 13.5

9. 62

10. .028

_____ _____ _____ _____ _____

C Multiply by 1,000.

11. 4.675

12. .098

13. 4.7

14. 183

15. 13.6075

_____ _____ _____ _____ _____

D Multiply.

16. 94.7 x 1,000

17. 8.3 x 100

18. .0732 x 10

_____ _____ _____

Check Registers

A *check register* is used to keep track of the deposits and checks written. The *balance* tells the amount of money in the account. Deposits are added to the account; checks written are subtracted. If there is a *service charge* for each check, it is also subtracted.

Example: Tom Ward's account had a balance of $309.71. He made a deposit of $150.00 and wrote a check for $62.95. What is the balance in his account? There is no service charge.

CHECK NO.	DATE	CHECKS ISSUED TO OR DESCRIPTION OF DEPOSIT	AMOUNT OF CHECK	AMOUNT OF DEPOSIT	BALANCE
		BALANCE BROUGHT FORWARD			309.71
	5/12	deposit		150.00	459.71
201	5/12	Marcy's	62.95		396.76

Tom's balance in his account is $396.76.

Check recorded   Deposit

A Complete each transaction and find the current balance.

1. Keesha Jones's checkbook balance was $216.47 on February 3. Her check register shows these transactions.

CHECK NO.	DATE	CHECKS ISSUED TO OR DESCRIPTION OF DEPOSIT	AMOUNT OF CHECK	AMOUNT OF DEPOSIT	BALANCE
		BALANCE BROUGHT FORWARD			216.47
621	2/3	Howard Co.	42.56		a.
	2/5	deposit		85.00	b.
622	2/8	C & P Telephone	45.15		c.
623	2/9	Bargain City	60.15		d.

2. On June 15, Janie Clark's balance was $703.22. Her check register shows these transactions.

CHECK NO.	DATE	CHECKS ISSUED TO OR DESCRIPTION OF DEPOSIT	AMOUNT OF CHECK	AMOUNT OF DEPOSIT	BALANCE
		BALANCE BROUGHT FORWARD			703.22
186	6/15	Equitable Bank	85.72		a.
	6/16	deposit		175.00	b.
187	6/18	History Book Club	24.95		c.
188	6/19	Suburban Propane	95.12		d.
	6/21	deposit		175.00	e.

3. Use the following information to complete the check register below.

Date	Payee	Amount of Check
8/2	Finer Foods	$65.18
8/3	Kelly's Meats	125.00
8/5	Provident Savings Bank	187.50
8/6	Thomas Bann	20.00
8/8	W. Ball & Co.	29.95
8/10	Bill's Hardware	48.16

CHECK NO.	DATE	CHECKS ISSUED TO OR DESCRIPTION OF DEPOSIT	AMOUNT OF CHECK	AMOUNT OF DEPOSIT	BALANCE
		BALANCE BROUGHT FORWARD			708.12
a.	7/25	deposit		150.00	
b.					
c.					
d.					
e.					
f.	8/7	deposit		150.00	
g.					
h.					

Rounding Decimals

Rules to Remember:

To round decimals, look to the right of the place to which you are rounding.

➤ If the digit is 5 or more, round up.

➤ If the digit is 4 or less, round down.

Examples:

Round 2.768 to the nearest whole number.

2.768
▲ Digit to the right is 5 or more. Round up.

2.768 rounded to the nearest whole number is 3.

Round 3.273 to the nearest hundredth.

3.273
▲ Digit to the right is 4 or less. Round down.

3.273 rounded to the nearest hundredth is 3.27.

A Round to the nearest whole number.

1. 8.3

2. 24.6

3. 32.38

4. 9.06

_____

_____

_____

_____

B Round to the nearest tenth.

5. .68

6. 3.73

7. .072

8. 13.628

_____

_____

_____

_____

C Round to the nearest hundredth.

9. .625

10. 4.769

11. .0692

12. 27.003

_____

_____

_____

_____

13. The cost of gasoline is 1.295 dollars per gallon. Round to the nearest cent.

_____

Percents to Decimals, Decimals to Percents

Percent means hundredths.

To change a percent to a decimal:

➤ Move the decimal point two places to the left.

➤ Drop the percent sign.

To change a decimal to a percent:

➤ Move the decimal point two places to the right.

➤ Insert a percent sign.

Examples:

Write a decimal for 27%.
27% = 27% = .27

Write a decimal for 5.4%.
5.4% = 05.4% = .054

Write a percent for .85.
.85 = .85 – 85%

Write a percent for .075.
.075 = .075 = 7.5%

A Write a decimal for each.

1. 28% _____

2. 80% _____

3. 3% _____

4. 12.5% _____

5. 98.62% _____

6. $5\frac{1}{4}$% _____

7. 9.5% _____

8. 12.678% _____

9. $2\frac{1}{2}$% _____

10. .4% _____

B Write a percent for each.

11. .65 _____

12. .165 _____

13. .08 _____

14. .1175 _____

15. .072 _____

16. $.62\frac{1}{2}$ _____

17. $.08\frac{1}{4}$ _____

18. .093 _____

19. .34 _____

20. .24 _____

Hourly Pay and Overtime

Many people are paid by the hour for the work they do. The *hourly rate* is the amount of money earned per hour. The *straight-time pay* is the amount of money earned for a pay period at the hourly rate. Employees who work more than eight hours in one day or more than forty hours in one week are paid at an *overtime rate.* This rate is usually 1.5 times the regular hourly rate and is called time and a half. The *gross pay* is the sum of the straight-time pay plus any overtime pay.

Example: Scott Jones works at the Crab Shack. Last week he worked 44 hours. His regular rate is $5.20 an hour. He is paid time and a half for all hours over 40. What is his gross pay for the week?

| Straight-Time Pay | = | Hours Worked | x | Hourly Rate |

= 40 x $5.20

= $208.00

| Overtime Pay | = | Hours Worked | x | Hourly Rate | x | Overtime Rate |

= 4 x $5.20 x 1.5

= $31.20

| Gross Pay | = | Straight-Time Pay | + | Overtime Pay |

= $208 + $31.20

= $239.20

Scott's gross pay is $239.20.

[artwork: restaurant]

A Find the gross pay. All hours over 40 are paid at the time-and-a-half rate. The regular rate is $5.40.

1. 24 hours _____

2. 50 hours _____

3. 60 hours _____

4. $27\frac{1}{2}$ hours _____

5. 48 hours _____

6. 72 hours _____

B Find the gross pay. The overtime rate is 1.5 times the regular hourly rate.

	Regular Hours	Straight-Time Rate	Straight-Time Pay	Overtime Hours	Overtime Pay	Gross Pay
7.	40	$5.30		2		
8.	36	5.45		6		
9.	40	6.10		8		
10.	38	5.25		5		
11.	40	6.15		12		
12.	40	7.35		8		
13.	36	6.80		10		
14.	40	7.20		12		
15.	40	6.50		20		
16.	30	5.15		10		

17. Rob is an electronics technician. Last week he worked 48 hours. His regular hourly rate is $9.50. What was his gross pay for the week? _____

18. Joan is a waitress. She worked 50 hours last week. She receives $5.00 an hour plus time and a half for overtime. In addition to her regular pay, she received $75.50 in tips. What was her gross pay? _____

19. Lucy works for the phone company as an installer. She worked 45 hours last week. She makes $10.75 per hour for the first 40 hours and time and a half for the remaining hours. What was her gross pay? _____

20. Sara is a nurse. She worked 42 hours last week. She receives $14.25 an hour plus time and a half for overtime—any hours over 38 hours per week. What was her gross pay? _____

Commissions

People who sell things are often paid a commission. A *commission* is a percent of the sales paid to the person making the sales. Some salespersons are paid a weekly salary plus a commission on their sales.

Example: Mike Johnson sells shoes. He is paid an hourly rate of $6.10 per hour and a commission of 5% on all his sales. Last week he worked 40 hours and sold $1,980 worth of shoes. What was his gross pay for the week?

| Straight-Time Pay | = | Hours Worked | x | Hourly Rate |

= 40 x $6.10

= $244.00

| Commission | = | Sales | x | Rate of Commission |

= $1,980 x .05

= $99.00

| Gross Pay | = | Straight-Time Pay | + | Commission |

= $244.00 + $99.00

= $343.00

Mike's gross pay is $343.00.

A Find the commission for each.

	1.	2.	3.	4.	5.	6.	7.
Sales	$300	$2,000	$1,500	$2,400	$1,800	$2,500	$400
Rate of Commission	15%	8%	4%	5%	$6\frac{1}{2}$%	$4\frac{1}{2}$%	6.3%
Commission							

8. Tom Troy is an auto mechanic. He receives a straight commission of 20% on the repair income that he brings in each week. What is his commission if he brings in $1,950 of repair income in a week? _____

9. Donna Magin is a car salesperson. She receives a straight commission of $2\frac{1}{2}$% of the selling price of each car. What commission will she receive for selling a $22,500 car? _____

B Find the gross pay for each.

	Hourly Rate	Hours Worked	Straight-Time Pay	Rate of Commission	Sales	Commission	Gross Pay
10.	$5.50	40		5%	$600		
11.	6.00	45		10%	1,000		
12.	6.35	40		12%	850		
13.	8.00	36		8%	550		
14.	5.00	40		$2\frac{1}{2}$%	2,000		
15.	6.50	40		3%	4,500		
16.	10.00	35		5%	2,500		
17.	5.10	40		$3\frac{1}{2}$%	4,000		
18.	9.00	25		6%	1,500		
19.	12.60	40		$4\frac{1}{2}$%	2,800		
20.	7.50	38		6%	3,200		

Gross and Net Pay

The sum of a person's earnings is called the *gross pay*. *Deductions* are the amounts subtracted from a worker's pay. They include items such as taxes, insurance, and union dues. The *net pay* or *take-home pay* is the amount received after the deductions have been subtracted.

Example: Karen earns $8.50 an hour. Last week she worked 36 hours. Her deductions were $32.75. What is her net pay?

Gross Pay	=	Hours Worked	x	Hourly Rate

   = 36 x $8.50

   = $306.00

Net Pay	=	Gross Pay	−	Deductions

   = $306.00 – $32.75

   = $273.25

Karen's net pay is $273.25.

A Find the net pay.

1. Gross pay: $182.75
   Deductions:
   Fed. withholding: $23.50
   F.I.C.A.: $13.05

   _____

2. Gross pay: $215.95
   Deductions:
   Fed. withholding: $30.95
   State tax: $10.15
   F.I.C.A.: $17.18

   _____

B Find the gross pay and net pay for each worker.

	Name	Hours Worked	Hourly Rate	Gross Pay	Deductions	Net Pay
3.	Elzer G.	36	$6.50		$48.50	
4.	Thomas F.	40	7.25		72.15	
5.	Janie C.	38	5.25		38.12	
6.	Alice B.	30	6.18		42.30	
7.	William M.	40	9.20		65.90	
8.	Raymond B.	40	5.65		27.90	
9.	William G.	36	10.25		128.65	
10.	Juan J.	24	8.10		32.75	
11.	Paul B.	40	9.15		72.81	
12.	Ling C.	32	7.45		50.80	
13.	Dorothy J.	40	6.95		83.20	

14. A salesclerk works 40 hours a week at $6.25 per hour. His deductions are $72.28. What are his net earnings? _____

15. A nurse worked 48 hours last week. Her regular rate is $22.50 an hour. She is paid time and a half for all hours over 40. Her deductions are $275.80. What is her net pay? _____

C Find the net pay.

16.

DEPT.	EMPLOYEE	CHECK #	WEEK ENDING	GROSS PAY	NET PAY
29	Vernon Freck	68621	9/24/—	$290.50	
TAX DEDUCTIONS				PERSONAL DEDUCTIONS	
FIT	FICA	STATE	LOCAL	MEDICAL	UNION DUES	OTHERS
47.60	18.78	9.32	—	1.75	——	—

17.

DEPT.	EMPLOYEE	CHECK #	WEEK ENDING	GROSS PAY	NET PAY
12	Lee Otts	71358	9/03/—	$375.10	
TAX DEDUCTIONS				PERSONAL DEDUCTIONS	
FIT	FICA	STATE	LOCAL	MEDICAL	UNION DUES	OTHERS
23.30	22.73	14.05	4.58	2.95	6.00	2.00

Budget Record

A *budget* is a plan for managing money. A well-planned budget is the key to wise spending. The first step toward managing your money is to keep a record of how your money is spent. At the end of the month, you can list your *expenditures* on a budget sheet. Expenses that change from month to month, such as food and utility bills, are called *variable expenses*. *Fixed expenses,* like rent, are those that remain the same each month. *Annual expenses,* such as taxes and insurance, are paid only once a year.

The Valis family has a monthly net income of $2,365. Last month's expenses are shown on the next page.

_____ 1. On what monthly expense does the Valis family spend the most money?

_____ 2. What is the total of their variable expenses?

_____ 3. On which of the monthly fixed expenses do the Valises spend the most?

_____ 4. What are their total monthly expenses?

_____ 5. In March, did the Valises stay within their budget?

A BUDGET RECORD FOR <u>The Valis Family</u>   DATE <u>March</u>

MONTHLY VARIABLE EXPENSES		MONTHLY FIXED EXPENSES	
Food	$ 365.00	Rent/Mortgage Payment	$ 800.00
Household Expenses		Car Payment	$ 225.00
Electricity	$ 45.00	Other Installments	
Heating/Air Cond	$ 60.00	Appliances	$ 00.00
Telephone	$ 25.00	Furniture	$ 52.00
Water	$ 18.50	Savings	$ 50.00
Other	$ 00.00	Emergency Fund	$ 20.00
Transportation		TOTAL	$ (1,147.00)
Gasoline/Oil	$ 52.00	**ANNUAL EXPENSES**	
Parking	$ 00.00	Life Insurance	$ 600.00
Tolls	$ 00.00	Home Insurance	$ 00.00
Repairs	$ 35.00	Car Insurance	$ 550.00
Other	$ 00.00	Medical Insurance	$ 2,600.00
Personal		Real Estate Taxes	$ 00.00
Clothing	$ 65.00	Other	$ 00.00
Credit Payments	$ 50.00	TOTAL	$ (3,750.00)
Gifts	$ 25.00	MONTHLY SHARE	
Contributions	$ 40.00	(Divide by 12)	$ 312.50
Entertainment		**MONTHLY BALANCE SHEET**	
Movies/Theater	$ 25.00	NET INCOME	
Sports	$ 00.00	(Total Budget)	$ 2,365.00
Magazines	$ 00.00	Variable Expenses	$ 920.50
Newspapers	$ 25.00	Fixed Expenses	$ 1,147.00
Dining Out	$ 90.00	Annual Expenses	$ 312.50
TOTAL	$ (920.50)	TOTAL MONTHLY	
		EXPENSES	$ (2,380.00)
		BALANCE	$ (−15.00)

Monthly Fixed Expenses

Annual Expenses ÷ 12 = $312.50

Total Monthly Expenses

Variable Expenses

Overspent by $15.00

The Valis family's total monthly expenses were $2,380.

Carol Jones is a schoolteacher. This is a record of her monthly expenditures.

| A BUDGET RECORD FOR | Carol Jones | DATE | November |

MONTHLY VARIABLE EXPENSES

Food ....$ 175.00

Household Expenses

    Electricity ....$ 50.00

    Heating/Air Cond ....$ 55.00

    Telephone......................$ 20.00

    Water.............................$ 5.00

    Other.............................$ 12.00

Transportation

    Gasoline/Oil....................$ 48.00

    Parking ....$ 120.00

    Tolls ....$ 00.00

    Repairs...........................$ 145.00

    Other.............................$ 00.00

Personal

    Clothing ....$ 160.00

    Credit Payments ....$ 60.00

    Gifts..............................$ 50.00

    Contributions..................$ 50.00

Entertainment

    Movies/Theater...............$ 25.00

    Sports............................$ 45.00

    Magazines ....$ 00.00

    Newspapers....................$ 20.00

    Dining Out ....$ 65.00

TOTAL...................................$_____

MONTHLY FIXED EXPENSES

Rent/Mortgage Payment.......$ 750.00

Car Payment ....$ 275.00

Other Installments

    Appliances.....................$ 00.00

    Furniture ....$ 48.00

Savings ....$ 500.00

Emergency Fund...................$ 250.00

TOTAL..................................$_____

ANNUAL EXPENSES

Life Insurance.......................$ 500.00

Home Insurance....................$ 00.00

Car Insurance.......................$ 525.00

Medical Insurance.................$ 2,500.00

Real Estate Taxes ....$ 00.00

Other...................................$ 00.00

TOTAL..................................$_____

MONTHLY SHARE

    (Divide by 12) ....$_____

MONTHLY BALANCE SHEET

NET INCOME

    (Total Budget) ....$ 3,400.00

Variable Expenses.................$_____

Fixed Expenses....................$_____

Annual Expenses ....$_____

TOTAL MONTHLY

EXPENSES ....$_____

BALANCE ....$_____

A Answer the following questions.

1. What is the total of Carol's variable expenses? _____

2. What is the total of her monthly fixed expenses? _____

3. What is the total of her annual expenses? _____

4. What is the monthly share of the annual expenses? _____

5. What is Carol's monthly net income? _____

6. What are her total monthly expenses? _____

7. Did Carol stay within her budget? _____

8. By how much did she overspend or underspend? _____

B Find the monthly share of each annual expense.

9. $720 _____   10. $660 _____

11. $1,140 _____   12. $1,026 _____

13. $907.20 _____   14. $3,444 _____

15. $2,640 _____   16. $504.48 _____

17. $880.80 _____   18. $1,176 _____

19. $564 _____   20. $2,448 _____

Preparing a Budget

The first step in preparing a budget is to keep a record of your expenditures over a period of time. At the end of several months, you will be in a better position to determine your spending patterns.

Example: Tyrone has a part-time job after school that pays him a monthly income of $600. A record of his expenditures for the last three months is shown below.

Budget Item	January	February	March	Average Expenditure
Food	$95	$97	$96	$96.00
Transportation	80	78	72	1.
Clothing	93	105	97	2.
Personal Items	75	82	79	3.
Entertainment	60	50	63	4.
Gifts, Contributions	42	47	49	5.
Savings	155	141	144	6.
Total Expenses	$600	$600	$600	7.

Find his average expenditure for food.

Average Expenditure	=	Sum of Monthly Expenditures	÷	Number of Months

$$= (\$95 + \$97 + \$96) \div 3$$

$$= \$288 \div 3$$

$$= \$96.00$$

Tyrone's average monthly expenditure for food is $96.00.

A Use the record above to find the average expenditure for each item in Tyrone's budget (#1–#6) and to find Tyrone's average monthly expenses (#7).

B This is a record of how the Heilmans spent their income for the last four months. The Heilmans' monthly income was $2,500. Find the average expenditure for each item in their budget and their average monthly expenses.

Budget Item	May	June	July	August	Average Expenditure
Mortgage Payment	$850	$850	$850	$850	8.
Food	515	460	420	440	9.
Clothing	185	192	168	135	10.
Transportation	140	125	200	160	11.
Entertainment	75	80	75	80	12.
Insurance	150	150	150	150	13.
Utilities	165	170	185	190	14.
Telephone	25	22	24	28	15.
Personal Items	55	42	39	62	16.
Gifts, Contributions	46	45	48	69	17.
Savings	294	364	341	336	18.
Total Expenses	2,500	2,500	2,500	2,500	19.

20. What are the net earnings for each of the four months recorded here? _____

21. What is the average monthly expenditure for food? _____

22. Items that stay the same in a budget are called *fixed expenses*. What items are fixed expenses in this budget? _____

_____

23. How much do the Heilmans save on average each month? _____

24. How much do the Heilmans spend on entertainment on average each month? _____

25. What is the average monthly expenditure for transportation? _____

Preparing a Budget Record Sheet

U N I T 2

A The Browns are a young couple with an eighteen-month-old child. They have a monthly net income of $3,100. Complete the budget record sheet on the next page to prepare a budget for the Brown family. Write the correct month for the date. Include the following information:

The Browns' budgeted amounts for monthly variable expenses are

food, $515	heating or air conditioning, $60
telephone, $22	cable TV, $48
gasoline and oil for the car, $75	parking, $20
repairs to car, $50	clothing, $85
credit payments, $75	gifts, $45
contributions, $50	movies and sports (including baby-sitting fees), $80
magazines and newspapers, $25	dining out, $70

Their monthly fixed expenses include

rent, $675	car payment, $250
savings, $200	furniture installment payments, $30
emergency fund, $70	

The Browns' budgeted amounts for annual expenses are

life insurance, $300	car insurance, $475
medical insurance, $2,800	medical expenses, $1,200

A BUDGET RECORD FOR _____   DATE _____

MONTHLY VARIABLE EXPENSES	MONTHLY FIXED EXPENSES
Food ....$_____	Rent/Mortgage Payment ....$_____
Household Expenses	Car Payment........................$_____
Electricity $_____	Other Installments
Heating/Air Cond ....$_____	Appliances ....$_____
Telephone........................$_____	Furniture ....$_____
Water...............................$_____	Savings................................$_____
Other...............................$_____	Emergency Fund ....$_____
Transportation...........................	TOTAL ....$_____
Gasoline/Oil....................$_____	**ANNUAL EXPENSES**
Parking ....$_____	Life Insurance ....$_____
Tolls................................$_____	Home Insurance ....$_____
Repairs............................$_____	Car Insurance ....$_____
Other...............................$_____	Medical Insurance ....$_____
Personal	Real Estate Taxes...................$_____
Clothing ....$_____	Other ....$_____
Credit Payments ....$_____	TOTAL ....$_____
Gifts................................$_____	MONTHLY SHARE
Contributions ....$_____	(Divide by 12)...................$_____
Entertainment...........................	**MONTHLY BALANCE SHEET**
Movies/Theater.................$_____	NET INCOME
Sports..............................$_____	(Total Budget)...................$_____
Magazines ....$_____	Variable Expenses ....$_____
Newspapers.....................$_____	Fixed Expenses ....$_____
Dining Out ....$_____	Annual Expenses....................$_____
TOTAL...................................$_____	TOTAL MONTHLY
	EXPENSES.............................$_____
	BALANCE................................$_____

Does the Browns' budget need to be revised? _____

Rules to Remember:

To multiply two decimal fractions:

➤ Multiply as with whole numbers.

➤ Count the number of places to the right of the decimal point in both factors.

➤ Beginning at the right, count the same number of decimal places in the product.

➤ Place the decimal point.

➤ Sometimes it is necessary to annex zeros in the product.

Examples:

Multiply: 6.7 x 2.35

```
    2.35    2 places
   x 6.7    1 place
    1645
    1410
   15.745   3 places
```
Place decimal point.

Multiply: .27 x .063

```
    .063    3 places
   x .27    2 places
    441
    126
   .01701   5 places
```
Annex zero.

A Find the products.

1. 42.5
    x 7

2. 18.65
    x 12

3. 1.16
    x 76

4. 18.2
    x 3.5

5. 42.6
    x .07

6. 184
    x .38

7. 65.8
    x 1.3

8. .869
    x .18

9. .036	10. 2.74	11. .374	12. 1.768
x .5	x .006	x .82	x .006

13. 48.30 x 15 = _____   14. 62.19 x 28 = _____

15. 2.98 x 7.8 = _____   16. .073 x 24 = _____

17. .068 x .05 = _____   18. .179 x .039 = _____

By selling food in large quantities, fast-food restaurants can keep their prices low and still make a profit. For some restaurants, the profit ratio may be as low as .015 ($1\frac{1}{2}$¢) on some items.

B Find the profit on each item. Multiply.

	Item	Number Sold	Profit Ratio	Profit
19.	Hamburger	876	.035	
20.	Cheeseburger	495	.05	
21.	Tuna sandwich	128	.075	
22.	Fish sandwich	264	.06	
23.	French fries	2,963	.055	
24.	Onion rings	215	.08	
25.	Meatball sub	116	.065	
26.	Steak sub	89	.09	
27.	Milkshake	1,215	.035	
28.	Soda	2,865	.05	
29.	Milk	2,344	.025	
30.	Coffee	1,998	.045	

Credit Card Purchasing

If you buy something and agree to pay for it at a later date, you are using *credit*. The most popular form of credit is using a *credit card*. Once a month, those who have charge cards receive a statement telling how much is due on their account. When you do not pay the full amount due, you have to pay a *finance charge*.

Example: Howard's unpaid balance from last month is $238.25. This month his purchases totaled $112.14, and he made a $50 payment. The finance charge was $2.18. What is the new balance in his account?

BILLING DATE   10/10

ACCOUNT NO.   J987 736 0025D

DEPT	DATE	DESCRIPTION	PURCHASES	REFERENCE #	
19	9/12	Housewares	$72.31	7064	
03	9/26	Sporting Goods	$39.83	8309	

PREVIOUS BALANCE	PAYMENTS/CREDITS	UNPAID BALANCE	NEW PURCHASES	FINANCE CHARGES	NEW BALANCE
$238.25	50.00	188.25	112.14	2.18	?

$$\boxed{\text{New Balance}} = \left(\begin{array}{c}\text{Previous} \\ \text{Balance}\end{array} + \begin{array}{c}\text{New} \\ \text{Purchases}\end{array} + \begin{array}{c}\text{Finance} \\ \text{Charge}\end{array}\right) - \boxed{\text{Payments}}$$

$$= (\$238.25 + \$112.14 + \$2.18) - \$50.00$$
$$= \$352.57 - \$50.00$$
$$= \$302.57$$

The new balance on Howard's account is $302.57.

A Find the new balance on each:

	Previous Balance	New Purchases	Finance Charge	Payment	New Balance
1.	$92.80	$108.15	$1.40	$50.00	
2.	125.75	87.29	1.87	100.00	
3.	480.16	95.62	6.95	75.00	
4.	600.08	216.20	8.78	55.00	
5.	1,728.40	224.76	26.12	200.00	
6.	875.25	209.72	12.75	250.00	
7.	3,255.21	398.28	49.65	375.00	
8.	75.60	94.78	1.12	75.00	
9.	507.23	114.86	7.12	50.00	
10.	1,255.17	86.28	22.50	100.00	

B What is the unpaid balance and new balance?

PREVIOUS BALANCE	PAYMENTS/CREDITS	UNPAID BALANCE	NEW PURCHASES	FINANCE CHARGES	NEW BALANCE
$419.92	25.00	11.	49.35	7.18	12.

PREVIOUS BALANCE	PAYMENTS/CREDITS	UNPAID BALANCE	NEW PURCHASES	FINANCE CHARGES	NEW BALANCE
$473.48	100.00	13.	237.46	7.28	14.

C Complete the missing parts of this credit statement.

BILLING DATE   08/30

ACCOUNT NO.   Q387 636 1026F

DEPT	DATE	DESCRIPTION	PURCHASES	REFERENCE #	Payments/ Credits
08	7/04	Menswear: Sport coat	$85.95	84028	
10	7/21	Payment			$50.00
08	7/23	Menswear: Men's slacks	$32.50	77027	
06	7/28	Cosmetics: Cologne	$12.50	87469	

PREVIOUS BALANCE	PAYMENTS/CREDITS	NEW PURCHASES	FINANCE CHARGES	NEW BALANCE	MINIMUM PAYMENT
$430.35	15.	16.	2.18	17.	$15.00

Installment Purchasing

Expensive items are often sold on the *installment plan.* Instead of paying the full price of the item at the time of purchase, the purchaser pays only a part of the price. This part is called the *down payment.* The remainder is paid in *monthly installments.* As with all credit purchasing, a *finance charge* is added to the cost of the item.

Example: Juanita purchased a television for $650. She had to pay 20% down and make 12 monthly installments of $46.85. What is the installment price? What is the finance charge?

Down Payment	=	Cash Price	x	% Down

$$= \$650.00 \times .20$$
$$= \$130.00$$

Installment Price	=	Down Payment	+	Total Installment Payments

$$= \$130 + (12 \times \$46.85)$$
$$= \$130.00 + \$562.20$$
$$= \$692.20$$

The installment price is $692.20.

Finance Charge	=	Installment Price	–	Cash Price

$$= \$692.20 - \$650.00$$
$$= \$42.20$$

The finance charge is $42.20.

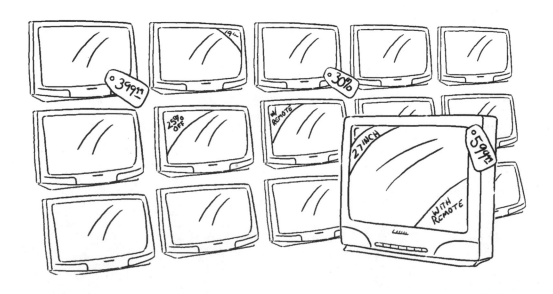

A Find the installment price and finance charge for each.

	Item	Cash Price	Down Payment	No. of Monthly Installments	Monthly Installment	Installment Price	Finance Charge
1.	Camera	$395	$95	12	$26.25		
2.	Color TV	875	150	6	135.50		
3.	Ring	525	85	18	27.15		
4.	Air conditioner	600	200	12	35.60		
5.	Boat	2,850	500	24	102.15		
6.	Lawn mower	290	75	6	38.65		
7.	Power saw	375	35	10	36.05		
8.	Camper	14,950	1,250	48	290.50		
9.	Refrigerator	900	275	18	36.40		
10.	VCR	395	60	20	18.75		
11.	Bedroom set	4,250	500	36	112.50		
12.	Motor	915	100	12	74.95		

B Find the down payment and amount financed.

	Item	Cash Price	Rate of Down Payment	Down Payment	Amount Financed
13.	Bed	$625	20%		
14.	Video camera	1,295	10%		
15.	Boat	1,800	15%		
16.	Color TV	995	30%		
17.	Telescope	165	12%		
18.	Microwave	450	20%		
19.	Sofa	895	10%		
20.	Air conditioner	720	25%		
21.	Camper	13,950	18%		
22.	Dishwasher	525	40%		

Short-Term Loans

Sometimes people need to borrow money for a short time to pay taxes, hospital bills, or an unexpected expense. Usually these loans are for a short period of time, six months to a year. A *finance charge* is added to cover the cost of borrowing the money.

Example: The Clearys had an emergency—the roof of their house needed to be repaired. They borrowed $2,000, which they plan to pay back in 6 monthly payments of $354.25. How much do they have to pay back? What is the finance charge?

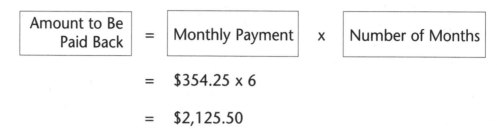

Amount to Be Paid Back	=	Monthly Payment	x	Number of Months

= $354.25 x 6

= $2,125.50

The amount to be paid back is $2,125.50.

Finance Charge	=	Amount Paid Back	−	Amount Borrowed

= $2,125.50 – $2,000.00

= $125.50

The finance charge is $125.50.

Find the amount to be repaid and the finance charge.

	Purpose	Amount Borrowed	No. of Payments	Monthly Payment	Amount Repaid	Finance Charge
1.	Landscaping	$2,000	12	$197.75		
2.	Taxes	1,800	6	324.80		
3.	Loan consolidation	950	10	109.25		
4.	College tuition	10,000	48	270.83		
5.	Hospital bill	28,500	36	820.20		
6.	Car repairs	400	6	71.65		
7.	Dental bill	2,200	12	212.65		
8.	Home remodeling	16,500	36	503.33		
9.	Business loan	5,000	18	311.35		
10.	Insurance	1,500	6	280.50		
11.	Home repairs	4,500	12	405.72		
12.	Car purchase	22,500	48	490.75		

13. Steve Cox borrowed $2,500 to pay for books for his first year at college. He will repay the loan in 24 monthly payments of $130.72. Find the amount paid back and the finance charge.

_____

_____

14. Tito Esteban borrowed $4,200 to remodel his kitchen. He made 36 monthly payments of $148.20. What was the amount repaid and the finance charge?

_____

_____

15. Mary Chang borrowed $1,800 to have her front yard landscaped. A finance charge of $135 was added to the amount she had to repay. If she pays off the loan in 12 monthly installments, how much will each payment be?

_____

Cost of Credit

An *installment loan* is a loan that is repaid in equal payments over a period of time. Included in the monthly payments is a *finance charge*. The finance charge is based on the amount financed, the number of monthly payments, and the *annual percentage rate* (APR).

APR	Term in Months	If You Finance			
		$200	**$500**	**$1,000**	**$1,500**
		Your Monthly Payment Is			
10%	6	34.31	85.78	171.56	257.34
	12	17.58	43.95	87.91	131.87
	18	12.01	30.02	60.05	90.08
	24	9.22	23.07	46.14	69.21
15%	6	34.80	87.01	174.03	261.05
	12	18.05	45.12	90.25	135.38
	18	12.47	31.19	62.38	93.57
	24	9.69	24.24	49.48	72.72
18%	6	35.10	87.76	175.52	263.28
	12	18.33	45.84	91.68	137.52
	18	12.76	31.90	63.80	95.70
	24	9.98	24.96	49.92	74.88

Example: Jim Robinson obtained a $1,500 installment loan to purchase furniture for his apartment. The annual percentage rate is 15%. He plans to repay the loan in 18 months. What is his monthly payment? How much is the finance charge?

At 15% for 18 monthly payments, the monthly payment is $93.57.

Amount Repaid	=	Monthly Payment	x	Number of Payments

    = $93.57 x 18
    = $1,684.26

Finance Charge	= $1,684.26 – 1,500.00

    = $184.26

The finance charge is $184.26.

A Use the table on page 44 to find the monthly payment.

1. Amount financed: $500
   APR: 15%
   Number of payments: 12

   _____

2. Amount financed: $1,000
   APR: 18%
   Number of payments: 18

   _____

3. Amount financed: $1,000
   APR: 18%
   Number of payments: 12

   _____

4. Amount financed: $200
   APR: 10%
   Number of payments: 6

   _____

B Find the monthly payment, the amount repaid, and the finance charge.

	Amount Financed	APR	Number of Payments	Monthly Payment	Amount Repaid	Finance Charge
5.	$200	10%	12			
6.	1,000	15%	18			
7.	1,500	10%	12			
8.	1,000	18%	24			
9.	500	10%	24			
10.	1,500	15%	18			
11.	1,000	15%	24			
12.	200	18%	6			
13.	1,500	10%	24			
14.	500	18%	12			
15.	1,000	15%	12			

16. The Fosters would like to obtain an installment loan of $1,500
    at an APR of 18% for 18 months. How much can they save by
    paying off the same loan in 6 months?   _____

UNIT 3

Rules to Remember:

To find a percent of a number:

➤ Write a decimal or a fraction for the percent.

➤ Multiply.

Examples:

Find 45% of 180.
45% = .45

$$\begin{array}{r} 180 \\ \times\, .45 \\ \hline 900 \\ 720 \\ \hline 81.00 \end{array}$$

45% of 180 = 81

Find $33\frac{1}{3}$% of 279.

$33\frac{1}{3}$% = $\frac{1}{3}$

$\frac{1}{\underset{1}{\cancel{3}}} \times \frac{\overset{93}{\cancel{279}}}{1} = 93$

$33\frac{1}{3}$% of 279 = 93

Find the percent of each number.

1. 25% of 64 _____

2. 30% of 72 _____

3. 80% of 600 _____

4. 12% of 95 _____

5. 4% of 75 _____

6. 15% of 240 _____

7. 8.5% of 80 _____

8. 48% of 65.5 _____

9. 1.8% of 250 _____

10. 37.5% of 80 _____

11. $33\frac{1}{3}$% of 54 _____

12. $66\frac{2}{3}$% of 360 _____

13. 72% of 25 _____

14. 50% of 24.80 _____

15. 5% of 280 _____

16. 62.5% of 128 _____

17. 3.5% of 400 _____

18. 12.5% of 480 _____

Dividing a Decimal by a Whole Number

Skill Building

Rules to Remember:

To divide a decimal by a whole number:

➤ Place the decimal point in the answer above the point in the dividend (number being divided).

➤ Divide as with a whole number.

➤ Sometimes it is necessary to place zeros in the answer.

Examples:

Divide: 9.12 ÷ 24

Decimal point in answer. ➤

$$
\begin{array}{r}
.38 \\
24\overline{)9.12} \\
-72 \\
\hline
192 \\
-192 \\
\hline
0
\end{array}
$$

Divide: 4.717 ÷ 89

Zero is placed in answer to show that 47 is not divisible by 89. ➤

$$
\begin{array}{r}
.053 \\
89\overline{)4.717} \\
-445 \\
\hline
267 \\
-267 \\
\hline
0
\end{array}
$$

 Divide.

1. $3\overline{)19.44}$

2. $15\overline{).795}$

3. $6\overline{)714.84}$

4. $7\overline{)4.48}$

5. $5\overline{).448}$

6. $9\overline{)177.3}$

7. $48\overline{)172.8}$

8. $16\overline{)757.44}$

9. $42\overline{).3612}$

10. $5\overline{)1.965}$

11. $12\overline{)22.32}$

12. $9\overline{).0846}$

Mid-Book Test

Definitions

A Read each definition. Write the letter of the word, phrase, or abbreviation that is being defined.

a. principal
b. compound interest
c. payee

d. commission
e. APR
f. passbook

g. gross pay
h. deductions
i. fixed expenses

j. finance charge
k. budget
l. hourly rate

_____ 1. expenses that remain the same each month

_____ 2. the record of a savings account

_____ 3. annual percentage rate

_____ 4. the amount of money earning interest

_____ 5. the person or company to whom a check is written

_____ 6. money subtracted from a paycheck

_____ 7. the cost of borrowing money

_____ 8. the interest earned on the original principal as well as on the interest earned during the previous interest period

_____ 9. a plan for managing money

_____ 10. the percent of a sale paid to the person who made the sale

Simple Interest

B Calculate the simple interest for each amount deposited in a savings account.

	Principal	Annual Rate	Time	Interest
11.	$1,500.00	8%	1 year	
12.	800.00	12%	18 months	
13.	8,500.00	4%	6 months	
14.	4,250.00	8%	9 months	
15.	625.00	4%	2 years	

Skill Check

C Make each of the following calculations.

16. Add: 17.85 + 6.094 + .414 = _____

17. Subtract: 7.85 − 3.268 = _____

D Multiply.

18. 15.21 x 10 = _____
19. .289 x 100 = _____
20. 4.3 x 10 = _____

21. 7.028 x 1,000 = _____
22. 2.89 x 100 = _____
23. .093 x 1,000 = _____

E Round to the nearest tenth.

24. 15.269 _____
25. .072 _____
26. 7.63 _____

F Write a decimal for each percent.

27. 43% _____
28. 88% _____

G Write a percent for each decimal.

29. .57 _____
30. .062 _____

Installment Purchases

H Find the down payment and the amount financed.

	Item	Cash Price	Rate of Down Payment	Down Payment	Amount Financed
31.	Calculator	$86.00	20%		
32.	Lamps	250.00	15%		
33.	Drapes	840.00	25%		
34.	Dryer	600.00	12%		
35.	Computer	2,200.00	15%		

Cost of a New or Used Car

New and used cars are advertised in the newspaper. The price advertised is not the total cost. For a new car, the *base price* is only the charge for standard equipment. There are extra charges for *options,* which are added features for safety, appearance, or convenience. There is a *destination charge* for shipping the car from the factory to the dealer. The total price of the car is called the *sticker price.* The state also has to be paid a sales tax and title and license plate fees.

Example: Ron Jason buys a new van. The base price is $22,550. Additional charges included $3,765 for options and a destination charge of $305. There is a 5% sales tax and title/license fees of $43. What is the total cost of the car?

Sticker Price	=	Base Price	+	Options	+	Destination Charge

$$= \$22{,}550 + \$3{,}765 + \$305$$
$$= \$26{,}620$$

Sales Tax	=	Sticker Price	x	Tax Rate

$$= \$26{,}620 \quad x \quad .05$$
$$= \$1{,}331$$

Total Cost	=	Sticker Price	+	Sales Tax	+	Title/License Fees

$$= \$26{,}620 + \$1{,}331 + \$43$$
$$= \$27{,}994$$

The total cost of the van is $27,994.

A Find the sticker price or total cost of each car.

1. Traveler
   Base price: $21,250
   Options: $2,625
   Destination charge: $225

   Sticker price: _____

2. Sunset Classic
   Base price: $22,400
   Options: $3,075
   Destination charge: $265

   Sticker price: _____

3. Range Rider
   Base price: $31,625
   Options/dest. ch.: $4,215
   Sales tax: $632
   Title/lic. fees: $45

   Total cost: _____

4. Matador
   Base price: $18,625
   Options/dest. ch.: $2,120
   Sales tax: $587.25
   Title/lic. fees: $38

   Total cost: _____

B Find the sales tax and total cost of each car.

	Base Price	Options/ Destination Charge	Sales Tax Rate	Sales Tax	Title/ License Fees	Total Cost
5.	$15,000	$3,750	4%		$65.00	
6.	20,500	2,850	5%		48.00	
7.	16,500	1,750	6%		35.00	
8.	21,200	2,695	4%		52.00	
9.	19,050	2,725	5%		38.75	
10.	17,865	1,975	6%		42.50	
11.	16,450	985	5%		27.00	
12.	19,450	2,865	4%		32.50	
13.	21,475	3,125	7%		45.00	
14.	23,650	3,700	6%		52.75	
15.	12,550	2,750	5%		43.50	

Financing a Car

U N I T 4

Financing a car is similar to buying on the installment plan. After a *down payment* is made, the amount left is paid in monthly installment payments. The sum of the down payment and the installment payments is called the *deferred-payment price,* or the actual total cost of the car.

Example: Frederico Panetta is buying a used car. The price of the car is $9,500. He makes a down payment of 20% and pays 24 monthly payments of $331. What is the amount to be financed? What is the deferred-payment price?

Down Payment	=	Price	x	Percent of Down Payment

= $9,500 x .20
= $1,900

Amount Financed	=	Price	–	Down Payment

= $9,500 – $1,900
= $7,600

The amount to be financed is $7,600.

Deferred-Payment Price	=	Down Payment	+	Total Installment Payments

= $1,900 + (24 x $331)
= $1,900 + $7,944
= $9,844

The deferred-payment price is $9,844.

A Find the down payment for each car.

1. Used midsize car
   Price: $7,850
   % down: 20%

   _____

2. New compact
   Price: $18,785
   % down: 10%

   _____

3. Used wagon
   Price: $9,075
   % down: 12%

   _____

4. Used small car
   Price: $10,275
   % down: 9%

   _____

5. New midsize car
   Price: $20,350
   % down: 15%

   _____

6. Used compact
   Price: $6,540
   % down: 8%

   _____

B Complete the chart and answer the problems.

	Price	Percent Down	Down Payment	Monthly Payments	Number of Payments	Total Payments	Deferred-Payment Price
7.	$8,500	15%		$ 312.25	24		
8.	17,950	20%		512.10	36		
9.	12,800	10%		595.00	20		
10.	26,150	25%		1,100.00	24		
11.	9,875	30%		156.50	48		
12.	13,500	8%		512.00	25		
13.	28,465	10%		482.20	60		
14.	18,600	12%		698.50	24		
15.	15,150	20%		854.20	18		
16.	7,875	18%		188.95	36		
17.	15,420	25%		244.75	50		
18.	14,300	11%		292.25	48		

19. Janet Webb is purchasing a new compact car with a sticker price of
    $20,500. She makes a down payment of 25% and 36 payments
    of $575.44. What is the deferred-payment price?   _____

20. Harvey Nickels purchased a used car with a cash price of $11,750.
    He traded in an older car valued at $2,500 and made 40 payments
    of $235.50. How much more did he pay than the cash price?   _____

Maintenance Costs

U N I T 4

Driving a car is expensive. Expenses, such as costs of gasoline, tires, and repairs, are called *variable expenses.* Expenses that remain the same—such as insurance, registration, and depreciation—are called *fixed expenses.* The annual expense of operating a car is often expressed in the cost per mile. To find the *cost per mile,* divide the annual expenses by the number of miles driven.

Example: John Kassouf drove 12,000 miles last year. His total car expenses were $3,120. What was the cost per mile to drive the car?

| Cost per Mile | = | Annual Expenses | ÷ | Miles Driven |

= $3,120 ÷ 12,000

= $.26

The cost to drive the car was $.26 per mile.

A Find the total expenses and the cost per mile.

	Annual Variable Expenses	Annual Fixed Expenses	Total Expenses	Miles Driven	Cost Per Mile
1.	$1,300	$1,500		10,000	
2.	1,120	1,200		8,000	
3.	1,580	1,660		12,000	
4.	2,290	2,510		20,000	
5.	1,855	1,895		15,000	
6.	1,725	1,125		9,500	
7.	2,675	2,897		18,000	
8.	1,572	1,702		10,000	
9.	1,899	1,995		21,000	
10.	1,030	1,150		8,000	
11.	2,100	2,280		19,000	
12.	985	1,210		5,000	
13.	2,415	1,520		15,000	
14.	1,010	2,000		25,000	

B The following table shows the estimated maintenance costs for a car over a period of six years.

Year	1	2	3	4	5	6
Maintenance costs	$200	$275	$360	$420	$600	$850

15. Martha's car is 3 years old. She drove her car 12,000 miles last year. Estimate her maintenance cost per mile for the third year. _____

16. Inez's car is 4 years old. She drove her car 7,000 miles last year. What was her maintenance cost per mile for the fourth year? _____

17. Karl drives 15,000 miles per year. His car is 5 years old. What was his maintenance cost per mile for the fifth year? _____

18. Last year Mohammed drove 17,000 miles. His car is 6 years old. What was his maintenance cost per mile for the sixth year? _____

19. Jim's car is 5 years old. In addition to maintenance costs, he had other expenses of $3,400. If he drove 16,000 miles last year, what was his cost per mile? _____

20. Maya took a 10,000-mile cross-country trip. She estimated her expenses to be $2,750. What was her cost per mile on the trip? _____

UNIT 4

Many states require that car owners carry insurance. Insurance policies contain these coverages:

Liability	Pays the cost of injury or damage for which the driver is at fault.
Collision	Pays for the damages to the driver's car due to an accident.
Comprehensive	Pays for the damages to the driver's car due to fire, theft, vandalism, or acts of nature.

Property Damage Limits	Bodily Injury Limits			
	15/30	25/100	50/100	100/300
$10,000	$90.50	$102.00	$105.50	$115.75
25,000	95.65	104.50	112.85	120.15
50,000	99.50	110.75	115.10	125.90
100,000	105.75	120.40	131.65	145.95

Insurance companies use tables such as this one to determine the premiums for liability insurance. Bodily injury limits of 15/30 means that the insurance company will pay up to $15,000 to any one person injured and up to $30,000 if more than one person is injured.

Example: Luis Torres has property damage coverage of $50,000 and bodily injury coverage of 50/100. The cost of collision and comprehensive insurance is $210. What is the total cost (premium) of his insurance?

$$\boxed{\text{Annual cost}} = \boxed{\begin{array}{c}\text{Cost of}\\\text{Liability Insurance}\end{array}} + \boxed{\begin{array}{c}\text{Cost of Collision/}\\\text{Comprehensive Insurance}\end{array}}$$

= $115.10 + 210.00

= $325.10

$115.10 is from the table.

The total cost (premium) is $325.10.

A Use the table on the opposite page to answer the questions.

1. John has $10,000 property damage coverage and bodily injury limits of 50/100 on his auto insurance. What is his premium for his liability insurance? _____

2. Lin has $50,000 property damage coverage and bodily injury limits of 25/100. What is his premium for the liability insurance? _____

3. Christa has $25,000 property damage coverage and bodily injury limits of 50/100. She also pays $275 for collision and comprehensive coverage. What is her total premium? _____

B Use the table on the opposite page to find the cost of liability insurance. Then find the total premium.

| | Coverages | | | | | |
	Property Damage	Bodily Injury	Liability	Collision	Comprehensive	Annual Premium
4.	$25,000	15/30		$170.25	$45.20	
5.	50,000	25/100		168.75	30.50	
6.	10,000	25/100		176.20	29.90	
7.	100,000	100/300		205.25	40.15	
8.	50,000	50/100		186.90	38.60	
9.	25,000	25/100		201.70	42.60	
10.	100,000	50/100		165.20	39.40	
11.	10,000	15/30		187.65	42.15	
12.	50,000	100/300		192.30	41.75	
13.	25,000	50/100		200.15	39.45	
14.	100,000	25/100		172.65	48.20	
15.	50,000	15/30		156.72	36.25	

Dividing a Decimal by a Decimal

Rules to Remember:

To divide a decimal by a decimal:

➤ Multiply both the divisor and dividend by 10, 100, or 1,000 to make a whole number divisor.

➤ Place the decimal point in the answer above the decimal point in the dividend after it has been moved.

➤ Divide as with whole numbers.

Examples:

Divide: 8.96 ÷ .32
The divisor is .32 (32 hundredths).
Multiply the divisor and the dividend by 100.

.32)8.96

$$
\begin{array}{r}
28 \\
32\overline{)896} \\
\underline{64} \\
256 \\
\underline{256}
\end{array}
$$

Move the decimal point two places to the right.

Divide: 3.6 ÷ .045
The divisor is .045 (45 thousandths).
Multiply the divisor and the dividend by 1,000.

.045)3.600

$$
\begin{array}{r}
80 \\
45\overline{)3,600} \\
\underline{360} \\
0
\end{array}
$$

Move the decimal point three places to the right.
Annex two zeros.

 Divide the following decimals.

1. $.4\overline{)3.76}$ 2. $.03\overline{).894}$ 3. $.8\overline{)1.912}$ 4. $35\overline{)22.05}$

5. $.12\overline{)2.232}$ 6. $.6\overline{)5.88}$ 7. $.09\overline{)4.59}$ 8. $.007\overline{)29.89}$

9. $.8\overline{)648}$ 10. $1.2\overline{)24}$ 11. $7.3\overline{)61.32}$ 12. $2.6\overline{)10.66}$

13. $.23\overline{)8.97}$ 14. $5.5\overline{)7.7}$ 15. $.7\overline{)28}$ 16. $2.9\overline{).464}$

17. 3.76 ÷ .04 = _____   18. 1.113 ÷ .7 = _____

19. .338 ÷ .13 = _____   20. .57 ÷ .006 = _____

21. .4316 ÷ .83 = _____   22. 9.482 ÷ 1.1 = _____

23. 8.5 ÷ .34 = _____   24. 4.50 ÷ 7.5 = _____

25. 42.12 ÷ 8.1 = _____   26. 1296 ÷ .54 = _____

27. .26 ÷ .004 = _____   28. 65.7 ÷ .09 = _____

29. Bonita purchased 13.5 gallons of gasoline for $17.28.
Find the cost per gallon.   _____

30. Joel purchased 10.75 yards of burlap for $16.34.
Find the cost per yard.   _____

Most people who buy a house pay part of the purchase price as a *down payment*. They take out a *mortgage loan* from a bank for the amount still unpaid.

Mortgage loans are repaid with interest in equal monthly installments over a period of time, usually from 15 to 30 years.

Example: The Klohr family bought a house for $180,000. They made a down payment of 20% of the purchase price and took out a 30-year mortgage for the rest. What is the down payment? What is the mortgage? Their monthly payments are $950.00. What is the total interest charged over the life of the loan?

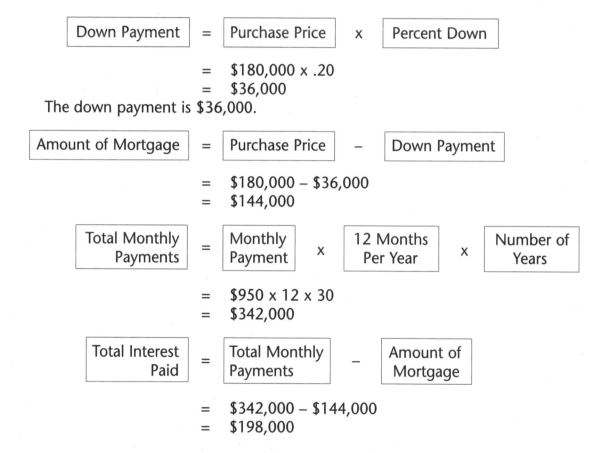

| Down Payment | = | Purchase Price | x | Percent Down |

= $180,000 x .20
= $36,000

The down payment is $36,000.

| Amount of Mortgage | = | Purchase Price | – | Down Payment |

= $180,000 – $36,000
= $144,000

| Total Monthly Payments | = | Monthly Payment | x | 12 Months Per Year | x | Number of Years |

= $950 x 12 x 30
= $342,000

| Total Interest Paid | = | Total Monthly Payments | – | Amount of Mortgage |

= $342,000 – $144,000
= $198,000

The total interest charged is $198,000.

A Find the down payment and the amount of the mortgage.

	Purchase Price	Rate of Down Payment	Down Payment	Amount of Mortgage
1.	$165,000	20%		
2.	185,000	10%		
3.	168,800	15%		
4.	92,500	25%		
5.	110,000	15%		

B Find the total of monthly payments.

	Amount of Mortgage	Length of Mortgage (Yr.)	Monthly Payments	Total Monthly Payments
6.	$125,000	15	$843.00	
7.	135,000	25	789.00	
8.	142,000	15	909.50	
9.	140,000	30	748.40	
10.	160,000	30	916.20	

C Find the total payments and the total interest paid.

	Mortgage	Length of Mortgage (Yr.)	Monthly Payments	Total Payments	Total Interest Paid
11.	$152,000	30	$712.35		
12.	140,000	15	960.40		
13.	137,500	20	888.50		
14.	160,000	15	1040.60		
15.	150,000	25	800.25		

Monthly Mortgage Payments

Tables similar to this one are used to find the amount of a monthly mortgage payment. The amounts in the table are for each $1,000 of the mortgage.

MORTGAGE LOAN SCHEDULE PER $1,000					
YEARS	9%	10%	11%	12%	13%
20	$9.00	$9.66	$10.33	$11.02	$11.72
25	8.40	9.09	9.81	10.54	11.28
30	8.05	8.78	9.53	10.29	11.06

Example: The Foster family obtained a $120,000 mortgage at a rate of 10%. They plan to pay it back in 30 years. Find the monthly payment and the total payments.

Find "30" under YEARS in the table and look to the right under 10%. The monthly payment is $8.78 per $1,000.

$$\text{Number of 1,000s} = \frac{120,000}{1,000} = 120$$

Monthly Payment	=	Monthly Payment per $1,000	x	Number of 1,000s

$$= \$8.78 \times 120$$

$$= \$1,053.60$$

The monthly payment is $1,053.60.

Total Payments	=	Monthly Payment	x	12 Months per Year	x	30 Years

$$= \$1,053.60 \times 12 \times 30$$
$$= \$379,296$$

The total payments are $379,296.

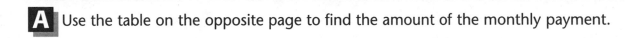
A Use the table on the opposite page to find the amount of the monthly payment.

	Amount of Mortgage	Rate of Mortgage	Length of Mortgage	Monthly Payment
1.	$135,000	9%	20	
2.	140,000	12%	25	
3.	127,000	13%	25	
4.	162,000	10%	30	
5.	185,000	11%	20	

6. Janet took out a 30-year mortgage for $150,000. The interest rate is 11%. What is the monthly payment? _____

7. Alberto obtained a 25-year mortgage for $120,000. The interest rate is 10%. What is the monthly payment? _____

B Find the monthly payment and total payments.

	Amount of Mortgage	Rate of Mortgage	Length of Mortgage (Yr.)	Monthly Payment	Total Payment
8.	$140,000	9%	25		
9.	225,000	12%	30		
10.	172,000	10%	20		
11.	166,000	9%	20		
12.	148,000	13%	25		
13.	228,000	10%	30		
14.	155,000	12%	25		
15.	120,000	11%	25		
16.	180,000	9%	30		
17.	200,000	11%	20		

Real Estate Tax

U
N
I
T
5

People who own their homes have to pay a tax based on the *assessed value* of the property. The assessed value is the value used for tax purposes. It is usually a percent of the *market value* (the selling price of the property on the open market). The real estate tax is based on the assessed value of the property and the *tax rate*.

Example: The Heilmans' house has a market value of $95,000 and is assessed for 65% of the market value. The tax rate is $3.80 per $100 of assessed value. What is the property tax?

Assessed value	=	Market Value	x	Rate of Assessment

$$= \ \$95{,}000 \times .65$$
$$= \ \$61{,}750$$

$$\text{Assessed value in 100s} = \frac{\$61{,}750}{100} = \ 617.5$$

Property tax	=	Assessed Value in 100s	x	Tax Rate

$$= \ 617.5 \times \$3.80$$
$$= \ \$2{,}346.50$$

The real estate tax is $2,346.50.

A Tell how many 100s are in each of the following.

1. $2,000 _____

2. $40,000 _____

3. $85,000 _____

4. $125,000 _____

5. $62,500 _____

6. $102,500 _____

B Find the assessed value of each of the following.

	Market Value	Rate of Assessment	Assessed Value
7.	$150,000	50%	
8.	160,000	60%	
9.	175,000	40%	
10.	220,000	45%	
11.	110,000	55%	

	Market Value	Rate of Assessment	Assessed Value
12.	$142,000	40%	
13.	180,000	62%	
14.	167,500	60%	
15.	145,000	55%	
16.	227,500	50%	

C Find the property tax.

17. Assessed value: $85,000
Tax rate: $6.00/$100

_____

18. Assessed value: $98,000
Tax rate: $4.50/$100

_____

19. Assessed value: $97,500
Tax rate: $3.80/$100

_____

20. Assessed value: $80,000
Tax rate: $5.75/$100

_____

D Find the assessed value and the property tax.

	Market Value	Rate of Assessment	Assessed Value	Tax Rate/$100	Property Tax
21.	$142,000	60%		$4.00	
22.	250,000	45%		4.40	
23.	175,000	40%		4.25	
24.	165,500	50%		6.20	
25.	112,000	45%		3.90	

Homeowners Insurance

In order to protect property against fire and other damage, *homeowners insurance* can be purchased. The amount of the premium depends on the amount of coverage, the material from which the house is constructed, and the quality of the fire protection.

YEARLY PREMIUMS

| Amount of Insurance Coverage | Brick/Masonry Veneer | | | | Wood Frame | | | |
| | Fire Protection Class | | | | Fire Protection Class | | | |
	1–6	7–8	9	10	1–6	7–8	9	10
$140,000	$406	$403	$528	$555	$438	$460	$555	$587
150,000	425	459	554	581	459	482	581	615
160,000	448	480	585	613	484	508	613	648
170,000	482	506	616	646	510	635	652	682
180,000	511	537	654	685	541	668	691	704
190,000	539	538	691	725	572	700	731	746
200,000	569	600	700	765	604	734	771	789
250,000	714	757	890	965	761	899	971	1,000

Example: The Fosters' house is brick and is rated in fire protection class 7–8. Find the yearly premium for homeowners coverage of $180,000.

Find $180,000 under "Amount of Insurance Coverage" in the table and look to the right under "Brick/Masonry Veneer" and then under "Fire Protection Class 7–8." The yearly premium is $537.

A Use the table on the opposite page to find the yearly premium for each policy.

	Amount of Policy	Type of Construction	Fire Protection Class	Yearly Premium
1.	$150,000	Wood frame	6	
2.	200,000	Brick	8	
3.	170,000	Brick	5	
4.	250,000	Brick	9	
5.	180,000	Brick	7	
6.	160,000	Wood frame	8	
7.	200,000	Wood frame	10	

8. The Smith family has coverage of $170,000 for homeowners insurance. Their house is a wood frame construction with a class 6 fire protection rating. What is the yearly premium?   _____

The table on the right shows the kinds of protection and the amount of the coverage provided by some homeowners policies.

Category	Coverage
Home	Full Policy
Personal property on premises	50% of policy
Additional structures	10% of policy
Additional living expenses	20% of policy
Personal liabilities	$35,000

B Use the table above to find the amount of coverage for each policy.

	Amount of Policy	Personal Property on Premises	Additional Structures	Additional Living Expenses
9.	$150,000			
10.	$140,000			
11.	$170,000			
12.	$180,000			
13.	$220,000			
14.	$250,000			
15.	$300,000			

What Percent One Number Is of Another

Rules to Remember:

To find what percent one number is of another:

➤ Divide the product by the second factor.

➤ Change the decimal to a percent.

Examples:

Find ____% of 60 = 36

Factor   **Product**

$$\begin{array}{r} .60 \\ 60\overline{)36.00} \\ \underline{360} \\ 0 \end{array}$$

60% of 60 = 36

Find ____% of 540 = 24.3

Factor   **Product**

$$\begin{array}{r} .045 \\ 540\overline{)24.300} \\ \underline{2160} \\ 2700 \end{array}$$

4.5% of 540 = 24.3

■ Find the percents.

1. _____ % of 60 = 30

2. _____ % of 20 = 15

3. _____ % of 72 = 36

4. _____ % of 25 = 5

5. _____ % of 75 = 25

6. 24 = _____ % of 40

7. 40 = _____ % of 60

8. _____ % of 64 = 16

9. _____ % of 20 = 17

10. 15 = _____ % of 60

11. 25 = _____ % of 80

12. _____ % of 50 = 12

13. _____ % of 40 = 3

14. 36 = _____ % of 72

15. 12 = _____ % of 40

16. _____ % of 16 = 6

17. _____ % of 50 = 19

18. 40 = _____ % of 75

19. 21 = _____ % of 70

20. 8 = _____ % of 25

Writing Fractions in Lowest Terms

Rules to Remember:

To write a fraction in lowest terms:

➤ Divide the numerator and denominator by a number that will divide each without a remainder.

➤ Repeat this until the numerator and denominator cannot be divided by the same number except 1.

Examples:

Write $\frac{25}{40}$ in lowest terms.

$\frac{25}{40} = \frac{25 \div 5}{40 \div 5} = \frac{5}{8}$ lowest terms

Write $\frac{24}{60}$ in lowest terms.

$\frac{24}{60} = \frac{24 \div 3}{60 \div 3} = \frac{8}{20}$ not in lowest terms

$\frac{8}{20} = \frac{8 \div 4}{20 \div 4} = \frac{2}{5}$ lowest terms

 Write each fraction in lowest terms.

1. $\frac{8}{16} =$

2. $\frac{9}{12} =$

3. $\frac{10}{25} =$

4. $\frac{4}{16} =$

5. $\frac{18}{24} =$

6. $\frac{5}{15} =$

7. $\frac{10}{15} =$

8. $\frac{28}{50} =$

9. $\frac{10}{12} =$

10. $\frac{12}{16} =$

11. $\frac{12}{24} =$

12. $\frac{18}{21} =$

13. $\frac{12}{36} =$

14. $\frac{15}{25} =$

15. $\frac{14}{28} =$

16. $\frac{20}{30} =$

17. $\frac{7}{21} =$

18. $\frac{28}{32} =$

19. $\frac{6}{16} =$

20. $\frac{34}{50} =$

21. $\frac{18}{45} =$

22. $\frac{50}{75} =$

23. $\frac{20}{25} =$

24. $\frac{24}{32} =$

25. $\frac{72}{90} =$

26. $\frac{5}{25} =$

27. $\frac{18}{90} =$

28. $\frac{21}{30} =$

29. $\frac{20}{32} =$

30. $\frac{24}{50} =$

Sales Tax

In most states, there is a tax on certain items that are purchased. The rate is not the same in all states. The amount of sales tax can be read from a table, or it can be computed.

6% SALES TAX SCHEDULE					
Transaction	Tax	Transaction	Tax	Transaction	Tax
.01–.10	.00	8.42–8.58	.51	16.92–17.08	1.02
.11–.22	.01	8.59–8.74	.52	17.09–17.24	1.03
.23–.39	.02	8.75–8.91	.53	17.25–17.41	1.04
.40–.56	.03	8.92–9.08	.54	17.42–17.58	1.05
.57–.73	.04	9.09–9.24	.55	17.59–17.74	1.06
.74–.90	.05	9.25–9.41	.56	17.75–17.91	1.07
.91–1.08	.06	9.42–9.58	.57	17.92–18.08	1.08
1.09–1.24	.07	9.59–9.74	.58	18.09–18.24	1.09
1.25–1.41	.08	9.75–9.91	.59	18.25–18.41	1.10
1.42–1.58	.09	9.92–10.08	.60	18.42–18.58	1.11
1.59–1.74	.10	10.09–10.24	.61	18.59–18.74	1.12
1.75–1.91	.11	10.25–10.41	.62	18.75–18.91	1.13
1.92–2.08	.12	10.42–10.58	.63	18.92–19.08	1.14
2.09–2.24	.13	10.59–10.74	.64	19.09–19.24	1.15
2.25–2.41	.14	10.75–10.91	.65	19.25–19.41	1.16
2.42–2.58	.15	10.92–11.08	.66	19.42–19.58	1.17
2.59–2.74	.16	11.09–11.24	.67	19.59–19.74	1.18
2.75–2.91	.17	11.25–11.41	.68	19.75–19.91	1.19
2.92–3.08	.18	11.42–11.58	.69	19.92–20.08	1.20
3.09–3.24	.19	11.59–11.74	.70	20.09–20.24	1.21
3.25–3.41	.20	11.75–11.91	.71	20.25–20.41	1.22
3.42–3.58	.21	11.92–12.08	.72	20.42–20.58	1.23
3.59–3.74	.22	12.09–12.24	.73	20.59–20.74	1.24
3.75–3.91	.23	12.25–12.41	.74	20.75–20.91	1.25
3.92–4.08	.24	12.42–12.58	.75	20.92–21.08	1.26
4.09–4.24	.25	12.59–12.74	.76	21.09–21.24	1.27
4.25–4.41	.26	12.75–12.91	.77	21.25–21.41	1.28
4.42–4.58	.27	12.92–13.08	.78	21.42–21.58	1.29
4.59–4.74	.28	13.09–13.24	.79	21.59–21.74	1.30

Example: Danielle Reid bought a skirt priced at $21.49. The sales tax rate is 6%. Find the sales tax using the chart. What is the sales tax when it is computed? What is the total cost of the skirt?

Using the tax table, $21.49 falls in the bracket $21.42–21.58, so the tax is $1.29.

Sales Tax	=	Tax Rate	x	Price

=   .06 x $21.49

= $1.2894 (rounded to the next highest cent = $1.29)

Note: Always round up for sales tax.

Total Price	=	Price	+	Sales Tax

= $21.49 + $1.29

= $22.78

The total cost of the skirt was $22.78.

A Use the sales tax table to find the sales tax on each amount.

1. $.85 _____

2. $1.72 _____

3. $4.27 _____

4. $8.47 _____

5. $19.45 _____

6. $13.10 _____

B Use the sales tax table to find the sales tax and the total cost on each item.

7. Tie: $20.79
   Sales tax _____
   Total cost _____

8. Pizza: $9.75
   Sales tax _____
   Total cost _____

9. Book: $9.95
   Sales tax _____
   Total cost _____

10. Plant: $13.15
    Sales tax _____
    Total cost _____

C Compute the sales tax and the total cost of each item.

	Item Purchased	Selling Price	Tax Rate	Sales Tax	Total Cost
11.	VCR	$349.50	4%		
12.	Refrigerator	995.00	6%		
13.	Pants	49.95	4%		
14.	Hair curler	17.50	5%		
15.	Flashlight	23.95	6%		
16.	Golf clubs	475.00	4%		
17.	Case of soda	16.50	5%		
18.	Motor	695.00	7%		
19.	Radio	47.95	6%		
20.	Ice cream	6.65	5%		

Social Security

F.I.C.A. tax is withheld from a worker's paycheck. This tax is also called the *Social Security Tax*. There are two parts to the F.I.C.A. tax—the tax rate and the maximum amount of income that is taxed.

Employers must match the amount paid by workers to social security.

Example:

In 1988, Janet earned $48,000. How much social security tax did she pay?

Year	Maximum Taxed	Employee Rate
1987	$43,500	7.15%
1988	$45,000	7.51%
1989	$46,600	7.51%
1990	$48,200	7.65%
1994	$60,600	6.20%

Since $48,000 is greater than the maximum pay taxed, only $45,000 is subject to the tax.

In 1988 the tax rate was 7.51%.

Social Security Tax	=	Gross Pay	x	Social Security Tax

$$= \$45,000 \times .0751$$
$$= \$3,379.50$$

7.51% = .0751

She paid a social security tax of $3,379.50.

A Use the table above to find the F.I.C.A. tax in each case.

	Year	Income	F.I.C.A. Tax
1.	1988	$16,500	
2.	1989	20,000	
3.	1987	42,600	
4.	1990	38,400	
5.	1994	18,750	

	Year	Income	F.I.C.A. Tax
6.	1987	$50,000	
7.	1994	25,500	
8.	1990	38,200	
9.	1989	65,000	
10.	1988	36,650	

11. In 1987, Stella Dawes earned $24,500. How much was deducted for Social Security? _____

12. A lawyer earned an income of $72,000 in 1990. What was his Social Security tax deduction? _____

Persons who are self-employed pay the entire Social Security tax. This tax is paid entirely by the employee.

Year	Maximum Pay Taxed	Employee Rate
1987	$43,500	14.30%
1988	45,000	15.02%
1989	46,600	15.02%
1990	48,200	15.30%
1994	60,600	12.40%

B Find the F.I.C.A. tax for these self-employed persons. Use the table above.

	Year	Income	F.I.C.A. Tax
13.	1988	$16,500	
14.	1989	20,000	
15.	1987	42,600	
16.	1990	38,400	
17.	1994	18,750	

	Year	Income	F.I.C.A. Tax
18.	1987	$50,000	
19.	1994	25,500	
20.	1990	38,200	
21.	1989	65,000	
22.	1988	36,650	

23. A pastor estimated his 1989 income as $35,700. Find his Social Security tax for the year. _____

24. A self-employed writer estimated that her 1990 income was $55,000. What was her Social Security tax? _____

25. An actor estimated that his 1988 income was $45,000. Find his Social Security tax for the year. _____

Adjusted Gross Income

Anyone who has taxes *withheld* from his or her pay receives a *Form W–2* in January. This form states the total earnings and federal and state taxes withheld during the previous year. This form is used to provide information for the income tax return.

The federal government taxes income. To find the *taxable income,* first find the adjusted gross income. The *adjusted gross income* is the sum of all wages, dividends, interest, tips, and other income earned during the year.

a Control number	22222	Void ☐	For Official Use Only ▶ OMB No. 1545-0008		
b Employer's identification number 10-000-2			**1** Wages, tips, other compensation 7,609.25		**2** Federal income tax withheld 827.16
c Employer's name. address. and ZIP code CRAB SHACK 1728 COASTAL HIGHWAY OCEAN CITY, MD 21403			**3** Social Security wages 7,609.25		**4** Social security tax withheld 544.06
			5 Medicare wages and tips		**6** Medicare tax withheld
			7 Social security tips		**8** Allocated tips
d Employee's social security number 216-08-7214			**9** Advance EIC payment		**10** Dependent care benefits
e Employee's name (first, middle initial, last) Michelle Flynn 113C New Lane Ocean City, MD 21043			**11** Nonqualified plans		**12** Benefits included in box 1
			13 See Instrs. for box 13		**14** Other

	15 Statutory employee ☐	Deceased ☐	Pension plan ☐	Legal rep. ☐	Hshld. emp. ☐	Subtotal ☐	Deferred compensation ☐
f Employee's address and ZIP code							

16 State MD	Employer's state I.D. No. 98-768-0	17 State wages. tips. etc. 7,609.25	18 State income tax 425.17	19 Locality name	20 Local wages. tips. etc.	21 Local income tax

Cat. No. 10134D

Department of the Treasury—Internal Revenue Service

Form **W-2** **Wage and Tax Statement** **1996**

For Paperwork Reduction Act Notice, see separate instructions.

Copy B to be filed with employee's FEDERAL tax return

Example: Michelle earned $7,609.25 at the Crab Shack. She also earned $175.00 a week for the 24 weeks she worked at the Food Lion and had $285.25 of interest income. What is her adjusted gross income?

$$\boxed{\text{Earnings}} = \boxed{\begin{array}{c}\text{Weekly Earnings} \\ \text{at Food Lion}\end{array}} \times \boxed{\begin{array}{c}\text{Number of Weeks} \\ \text{Worked}\end{array}}$$

$$= \$175.00 \times 24$$
$$= \$4,200$$

$$\boxed{\text{Adjusted Gross Income}} = \boxed{\text{Wages}} + \boxed{\text{Interest Income}}$$

$$= (\$7,609.25 + \$4,200.00) + \$285.25$$
$$= \$11,809.25 + \$285.25$$
$$= \$12,094.50$$

The adjusted gross income is $12,094.50.

Find the adjusted gross income for the year.

1. Weekly wage: $620
   Interest income: $725.50

2. Weekly wage: $495.50
   Commissions: $985.60
   Interest income: $184.90

3. Monthly income: $2,075.00
   Part-time job: $865.00

4. Monthly income: $2,295
   Interest income: $865.90

5. Scott Jones earned $475 per week during the 12 weeks he worked during the summer. He also had a part-time job for 30 weeks and earned $315 per week. What was his adjusted gross income?

6. Maria worked in a shoe store where she earned $6.25 per hour. She worked 40 hours per week for 30 weeks. What was her adjusted gross income?

UNIT 6

Taxable income is equal to adjusted gross income less *deductions* and the *allowance for exemptions*. Deductions are allowed for medical expenses, taxes paid, and contributions. A $2,500 exemption is allowed for each dependent.

| Taxable Income | = | Adjusted Gross Income | − (| Deductions | + | Allowance for Exemptions |) |

Example: Keith Kolbe has adjusted gross income of $37,500. His allowable deductions are $4,820 and he claims 2 exemptions. What is his taxable income?

| Taxable Income | = | Adjusted Gross Income | − (| Deductions | + | Allowance for Exemptions |) |

= $37,500 − ($4,820 + $5,000)
= $37,500 − $9,820
= $27,680   **2 x $2,500**

Keith's taxable income is $27,680.

A Find the taxable income.

1. Carla Sanchez
   Adjusted gross income: $51,250
   Deductions: $3,180
   Number of exemptions: 1

   _____

2. Bill Gerardi
   Adjusted gross income: $32,800
   Deductions: $7,950
   Number of exemptions: 3

   _____

3. Janice Allen
   Adjusted gross income: $46,500
   Deductions: $4,950
   Number of exemptions: 3

   _____

4. Chang Ho
   Adjusted gross income: $58,250
   Deductions: $7,895
   Number of exemptions: 4

   _____

B Find the amount allowed for exemptions and the taxable income.

	Adjusted Gross Income	Total Deductions	No. of Exemptions	Amount Allowed for Exemptions	Taxable Income
5.	$39,600	$4,275	2		
6.	54,275	3,600	3		
7.	30,600	4,928	1		
8.	36,170	2,895	3		
9.	55,000	10,745	2		
10.	27,900	6,075	1		
11.	52,450	4,125	3		
12.	63,875	13,795	4		
13.	70,100	3,612	2		
14.	46,900	12,495	5		
15.	24,515	3,126	0		
16.	20,158	2,561	1		

17. Karen Meushaw earned $40,950 in wages and had an investment income of $4,275. She had deductions of $6,035 and claimed 2 exemptions. What is her taxable income? _____

18. Gerard Carter has an income of $48,900. His wife earns $32,420. They file a joint return (combined incomes) and claim $15,900 in deductions. They have 3 exemptions. What is their taxable income? _____

19. Julia Wong earned $33,260 in wages. She had $4,516 in deductions and claimed 1 exemption. What is her taxable income? _____

20. Rosa Alvarez has an income of $26,500. Her husband earns $24,800. They file a joint return, claiming $8,750 in deductions and 4 exemptions. What is their taxable income? _____

Most states have an income tax. The difference between federal and state income tax is the tax rate. Part of a sample *tax rate schedule* for state income taxes is shown below.

Tax Rate Schedule

If taxable income is		Amount of Tax
over	**but not over**	
13,000	15,000	690 plus 9% of excess over 13,000
15,000	17,000	860 plus 10% of excess over 15,000
17,000	19,000	1,060 plus 11% of excess over 17,000
19,000	21,000	1,280 plus 12% of excess over 19,000
21,000	23,000	1,520 plus 13% of excess over 21,000
23,000		1,780 plus 14% of excess over 23,000

Example:　　Cindy Green's taxable income is $19,580. How much state income tax does she have to pay?

In the tax rate schedule, read down the "taxable income" column until you reach the bracket 19,000–21,000.

Read the tax at the right: 1,280 plus 12% of excess over 19,000.

Excess over $19,000　　=　　$19,580 – $19,000

　　　　　　　　　　　　=　　$580

Find 12% of $580:　　.12 x $580 = $69.60

　　　　| Total Tax |　=　　$1,280 + $69.60

　　　　　　　　　　　　=　　$1,349.60

Cindy's state income tax is $1,349.60.

A Find the state income tax. Use the tax rate schedule on page 78.

	Taxable Income	Tax
1.	$15,600	
2.	13,750	
3.	20,200	
4.	19,750	

	Taxable Income	Tax
5.	$21,900	
6.	22,500	
7.	24,000	
8.	52,000	

9. Steve Cox's taxable income was $18,690. What was his state income tax? _____

10. Keesha Carter had a yearly taxable income of $25,000. How much is her state income tax? _____

In some states, you can read the state income tax directly from a table. A portion of a state income tax table is shown here.

AND THE NUMBER OF EXEMPTIONS IS:

AT LEAST	BUT NOT MORE THAN	1	2	3	4	5	6	7	8	9	10
		YOUR TAX (Line 12) IS:									
17,300	17,399	693	653	613	573	533	493	453	413	373	333
17,400	17,499	698	658	618	578	538	498	458	418	378	338
17,500	17,599	703	663	623	583	543	503	463	423	383	343
17,600	17,699	708	668	628	588	548	508	468	428	388	348
17,700	17,799	713	673	633	593	553	513	473	433	393	353
17,800	17,899	718	678	638	598	558	518	478	438	398	358
17,900	17,999	723	683	643	603	563	523	483	443	403	363
18,000	18,099	728	688	648	608	568	528	488	448	408	368
18,100	18,199	733	693	653	613	573	533	493	453	413	373
18,200	18,299	738	698	658	618	578	538	498	458	418	378

B Find the state income tax. Use the tax table above.

	Taxable Income	No. of Exemptions	Tax
11.	$17,325	3	
12.	17,925	4	
13.	18,128	3	
14.	17,922	2	

	Taxable Income	No. of Exemptions	Tax
15.	$18,075	1	
16.	17,325	4	
17.	17,615	5	
18.	18,230	2	

Addition and Subtraction of Fractions

Rules to Remember:

To add or subtract fractions:

➤ Find the least common denominator (L.C.D.).

➤ Use the L.C.D. to write like fractions.

➤ Add or subtract numerators.

➤ Write the sum or difference over the common denominator.

➤ Write the answer in lowest terms.

Examples:

Add: $\frac{3}{4} + \frac{2}{3}$

L.C.D. = 12

$\frac{3}{4} = \frac{9}{12}$ ⟵ $\frac{3}{4} \times \frac{3}{3}$

$+ \frac{2}{3} = \frac{8}{12}$ ⟵ $\frac{2}{3} \times \frac{4}{4}$

$\frac{17}{12} = 1\frac{5}{12}$ ⟵ lowest terms

Subtract: $\frac{7}{10} - \frac{1}{3}$

L.C.D. = 30

$\frac{7}{10} = \frac{21}{30}$ ⟵ $\frac{7}{10} \times \frac{3}{3}$

$- \frac{1}{3} = \frac{10}{30}$ ⟵ $\frac{1}{3} \times \frac{10}{10}$

$\frac{11}{30}$ ⟵ lowest terms

A Add the following fractions. Write the answers in lowest terms.

1. $\frac{2}{3} + \frac{1}{6} =$

2. $\frac{1}{4} + \frac{1}{2} =$

3. $\frac{3}{4} + \frac{1}{4} =$

4. $\frac{3}{8} + \frac{1}{4}$

5. $\frac{5}{6} + \frac{2}{3} =$

6. $\frac{1}{2} + \frac{3}{4} =$

7. $\frac{5}{8} + \frac{3}{4} =$

8. $\frac{1}{3} + \frac{1}{6} =$

9. $\frac{3}{4} + \frac{5}{12} =$

10. $\frac{1}{6} + \frac{7}{12} =$

11. $\frac{2}{3} + \frac{3}{4} =$

12. $\frac{7}{8} + \frac{1}{2} =$

13. $\frac{2}{3} + \frac{5}{12} =$

14. $\frac{1}{5} + \frac{3}{10} =$

15. $\frac{2}{3} + \frac{1}{8} =$

16. $\frac{3}{8} + \frac{2}{3} =$

17. $\frac{5}{6} + \frac{1}{3} =$

18. $\frac{9}{10} + \frac{4}{5} =$

B Subtract the following fractions. Write the answers in lowest terms.

19. $\frac{3}{4} - \frac{1}{2} =$

20. $\frac{5}{8} - \frac{1}{4} =$

21. $\frac{2}{3} - \frac{1}{6} =$

22. $\frac{7}{8} - \frac{3}{4} =$

23. $\frac{15}{16} - \frac{3}{4} =$

24. $\frac{5}{12} - \frac{1}{4} =$

25. $\frac{1}{2} - \frac{1}{6} =$

26. $\frac{1}{2} - \frac{1}{3} =$

27. $\frac{3}{4} - \frac{1}{3} =$

28. $\frac{9}{10} - \frac{3}{5} =$

29. $\frac{7}{8} - \frac{2}{3} =$

30. $\frac{11}{12} - \frac{3}{4} =$

31. $\frac{9}{16} - \frac{1}{2} =$

32. $\frac{11}{32} - \frac{1}{8} =$

33. $\frac{7}{15} - \frac{1}{3} =$

34. $\frac{3}{4} - \frac{1}{12} =$

35. $\frac{15}{16} - \frac{7}{8} =$

36. $\frac{7}{12} - \frac{1}{2} =$

37. It took Lenny $\frac{1}{2}$ hour to walk to school and $\frac{3}{4}$ hour to walk home. How long did it take him to go to and from school? _____

38. Karen spent $\frac{1}{4}$ hour preparing for her science test and $\frac{7}{8}$ hour doing her algebra. How much time did she spend on her studies? _____

Certificates of Deposit

Certificates of deposit are a popular way of investing money. They usually earn interest at a higher rate than a regular savings account. Certificates may be purchased from the bank for amounts such as $500 and $1,000. The money must be left on deposit for a specified period, a time ranging from 3 months to 8 years. This table shows interest earned on each $1.00 invested for different periods of time.

AMOUNT PER $1.00 INVESTED, DAILY COMPOUNDING

ANNUAL RATE	INTEREST PERIOD					
	3 MONTHS	1 YEAR	2.5 YEARS	4 YEARS	6 YEARS	8 YEARS
5.75%	1.014278	1.059180	1.154458	1.258577	1.411952	1.584017
6.00%	1.014903	1.061831	1.161820	1.271224	1.433287	1.616011
6.25%	1.015529	1.064489	1.169103	1.283998	1.454945	1.648651
6.50%	1.016155	1.067153	1.176431	1.296900	1.476930	1.681950
6.75%	1.016782	1.069824	1.183806	1.309932	1.499246	1.715921
7.00%	1.017408	1.072501	1.191226	1.323094	1.521900	1.750579
7.25%	1.018036	1.075185	1.198693	1.336389	1.544896	1.785936
7.50%	1.018663	1.077876	1.206207	1.349817	1.568240	1.822006
7.75%	1.019291	1.080573	1.213768	1.363380	1.591936	1.858806
8.00%	1.019920	1.083278	1.221376	1.377079	1.615989	1.896348

Example: Martha Dungey bought a certificate of deposit for $4,000. It earned interest at the annual rate of 7.25%. How much interest will it earn in 4 years?

Amount at Maturity	=	Original Principal	x	Amount per $1.00

= $4,000 x 1.336389
= $5,345.56 (rounded to nearest cent)

Interest	=	Amount at Maturity	–	Original Investment

= $5,345.56 – $4,000.00
= $1,345.56

The interest earned is $1,345.56.

A Use the table on the opposite page to find the amount at maturity of each certificate of deposit.

1. Principal: $2,000
   Annual rate: 7.5%
   Interest period: 1 year

   _____

2. Principal: $5,000
   Annual rate: 6.75%
   Interest period: 2.5 years

   _____

3. Principal: $4,500
   Annual rate: 6.5%
   Interest period: 6 years

   _____

4. Principal: $20,000
   Annual rate: 8%
   Interest period: 3 months

   _____

B Complete the following chart.

	Principal	Interest Period	Annual Rate	Amount per $1.00	Amount at Maturity	Interest
5.	$1,000	1 year	6.00%			
6.	500	2.5 years	7.25%			
7.	2,500	8 years	6.75%			
8.	4,000	4 years	7.50%			
9.	5,500	3 months	7.00%			
10.	7,000	6 years	7.75%			
11.	3,500	4 years	6.00%			
12.	6,000	6 years	8.00%			
13.	8,500	4 years	6.75%			
14.	2,000	8 years	7.25%			
15.	12,000	3 months	8.00%			

16. Robert Cox bought a $5,000 certificate of deposit with an annual interest rate of 7.75%. The interest period was 4 years. What was the value of the certificate at maturity? How much interest did he earn?   _____

   _____

Buying and Selling Stock

Another method of investing money is to buy *shares of stock.* Owners of shares of stock are part owners of the corporation issuing the stock. People buy stock for the dividends it pays and for the profits they hope to make if they can sell the stock later at a higher price.

The amount you pay for stock depends on the cost per share, the number of shares you buy, and the *stockbroker's commission* (charge). Stock prices are listed daily in the newspaper.

New York Stock Exchange							
Name	Div	Pe	Sales	High	Low	Last	Chg.
ADT	.92	17	109	$30\frac{7}{8}$	$30\frac{1}{2}$	$30\frac{1}{2}$	$-\frac{3}{8}$
Advest	.12	9	43	$12\frac{7}{8}$	$12\frac{1}{2}$	$12\frac{7}{8}$	$+\frac{1}{8}$
AMD	—	—	981	21	20	$20\frac{3}{4}$	$-\frac{1}{4}$
Avon	1.00	14	875	$32\frac{1}{8}$	31	$31\frac{1}{4}$	$+1$
Ball	.82	17	210	$43\frac{1}{4}$	43	$43\frac{1}{4}$	—
BaltGE	1.90	10	785	$30\frac{1}{2}$	30	$30\frac{1}{8}$	$+\frac{1}{8}$
BkNYs	1.68	8	491	$41\frac{1}{2}$	$40\frac{3}{4}$	$41\frac{1}{2}$	$+\frac{1}{8}$
Banner	.06	11	31	22	$21\frac{3}{4}$	$21\frac{3}{4}$	$-\frac{1}{4}$
Bard	.40	24	898	$44\frac{7}{8}$	44	$44\frac{3}{4}$	$+\frac{7}{8}$
BASIX	.16	—	862	$7\frac{1}{2}$	$7\frac{3}{8}$	$7\frac{3}{8}$	$+\frac{1}{8}$
BMC	—	—	16	8	$7\frac{1}{8}$	8	—
Cenvill	2.20	9	22	$20\frac{1}{2}$	20	$20\frac{1}{4}$	$-\frac{1}{4}$
ChamSp	—	—	285	15	14	$14\frac{3}{4}$	$-\frac{3}{8}$
Chase	2.16	6	1923	$39\frac{5}{8}$	39	$39\frac{5}{8}$	$+\frac{3}{8}$

Example: Malcolm Carter purchased 100 shares of ADT at $30\frac{1}{2}$ per share. The stockbroker's commission was $34.75. What was the total amount Malcolm paid for the stock?

| Cost of Stock | = | Number of Shares | x | Cost per Share |

= 100 x $30.50 $\frac{1}{2} = .50$
= $3,050

| Total Amount Paid | = | Cost of Stock | + | Broker's Commission |

= $3,050.00 + $34.75
= $3,084.75

The amount Malcolm paid for the stock was $3,084.75.

A Find the cost of these shares of stock.

1. Charles Wildner
   Number of shares: 100
   Cost per share: $37\frac{1}{2}$

   _____

2. Juan Augusto
   Number of shares: 200
   Cost per share: $24\frac{3}{4}$

   _____

3. Janet Webb
   Number of shares: 500
   Cost per share: $42\frac{1}{2}$

   _____

4. Mary Uhland
   Number of shares: 850
   Cost per share: $18\frac{1}{4}$

   _____

B Find the cost per share, the cost of stock, and the total amount paid for these shares of stock. Use the *last price* on the chart on the opposite page for the cost per share. Change fractions to decimals: $30\frac{1}{8} = 30.125$

	Name of Stock	Cost per Share	Number of Shares	Cost of Stock	Broker's Charge	Total Amt. Paid
5.	BMC		600		$84.75	
6.	Chase		400		70.90	
7.	Avon		150		41.65	
8.	Banner		50		20.15	
9.	ADT		100		32.95	
10.	Bard		1,200		147.25	
11.	Balt GE		250		61.75	
12.	Cenvill		2,000		210.00	
13.	Advest		200		48.20	
14.	Ball		1,000		130.60	
15.	BASIX		750		92.80	
16.	Champ SP		1,000		125.15	

17. Dr. Jones purchased 200 shares of BYT stock at $41\frac{1}{2}$. The stockbroker's charge was $53.90. What was the total cost of the stock? _____

18. Ms. Carrera purchased 500 shares of ACO stock at $25\frac{1}{2}$. The stockbroker's charge was $135.50. What was the total cost of the stock? _____

Example: Later, Malcolm sold his 100 shares of ADT for 35 a share. The stockbroker's commission was $27.95. How much profit did Malcolm make?

$$\boxed{\text{Amount Received}} = \boxed{\begin{array}{c}\text{Number of}\\\text{Shares}\end{array}} \times \boxed{\begin{array}{c}\text{Selling}\\\text{Price}\end{array}} - \boxed{\text{Commission}}$$

$$= (100 \times \$35) - \$27.95$$

$$= \$3,500 - \$27.95$$

$$= \$3,472.05$$

$$\boxed{\text{Profit}} = \boxed{\text{Amount Received}} - \boxed{\text{Total Amount Paid}}$$

$$= \$3,472.05 - \$3,084.75$$

$$= \$387.30$$

Malcolm's profit was $387.30.

C Find the amount received and the profit.

	Number of Shares	Selling Price	Commission	Amount Received	Total Amount Paid	Profit
19.	200	$13\frac{1}{2}$	$36.50		$2,425.42	
20.	100	$26\frac{1}{4}$	22.75		2,441.25	
21.	300	$10\frac{1}{2}$	42.50		2,886.52	
22.	250	24	35.90		5,811.75	
23.	400	$42\frac{1}{2}$	85.25		16,270.90	

24. Cindy paid $12\frac{1}{2}$ per share for 200 shares of AXT stock. The commission was $48.75. Two years later she sold the shares for $16\frac{3}{4}$ per share and paid a commission of $50.35. How much profit did she make? _____

25. Rob paid $20\frac{1}{4}$ per share for 150 shares of Enon stock with a commission of $36.50. Three years later he sold the shares for $22\frac{1}{2}$ per share, paying a commission of $44.75. How much profit did he make? _____

Rules to Remember:

To write a fraction as a percent:

➤ Divide the numerator by the denominator. Carry the division to two places or more.

➤ Write a percent for the decimal.

Examples:

Write $\frac{25}{40}$ as a percent.

$\frac{25}{40}$ means $25 \div 40$

$$\begin{array}{r} .625 = 62.5\% \\ 40\overline{)25.000} \\ \underline{240} \\ 100 \\ \underline{80} \\ 200 \\ \underline{200} \end{array}$$

$\frac{25}{40} = .625 = 62.5\%$

Write $\frac{12}{18}$ as a percent.

$\frac{12}{18}$ means $12 \div 18$

$$\begin{array}{r} .66\frac{12}{18} = .66\frac{2}{3} = 66\frac{2}{3}\% \\ 18\overline{)12.00} \\ \underline{108} \\ 120 \\ \underline{108} \\ 12 \end{array}$$

$\frac{12}{18} = .66\frac{2}{3} = 66\frac{2}{3}\%$

■ Write a percent for each fraction.

1. $\frac{1}{4} =$

2. $\frac{2}{5} =$

3. $\frac{1}{2} =$

4. $\frac{1}{8} =$

5. $\frac{7}{20} =$

6. $\frac{3}{4} =$

7. $\frac{9}{10} =$

8. $\frac{3}{8} =$

9. $\frac{8}{25} =$

10. $\frac{9}{50} =$

11. $\frac{7}{40} =$

12. $\frac{1}{3} =$

13. $\frac{19}{20} =$

14. $\frac{7}{10} =$

15. $\frac{3}{40} =$

16. $\frac{9}{25} =$

17. $\frac{5}{8} =$

18. $\frac{5}{6} =$

19. $\frac{4}{5} =$

20. $\frac{7}{8} =$

21. $\frac{3}{5} =$

22. $\frac{11}{20} =$

23. $\frac{2}{3} =$

24. $\frac{16}{25} =$

25. $\frac{28}{40} =$

Bonds are sold on the market just as stock is. Many corporations raise money by selling bonds. When you purchase a bond, you are lending money to the corporation. The price of a bond is given as a percent of the *face value* that is printed on the bond. Bondholders receive interest on their bonds based on the face value.

Example: Find the cost of $2,000 worth of PBC bonds, which sold for $65\frac{1}{2}$%. How much interest would Leon expect to receive if the annual rate of return is $4\frac{1}{2}$%?

$$\boxed{\text{Cost of Bond}} = \boxed{\text{Face Value}} \quad \text{x} \quad \boxed{\text{Percent of Face}}$$

$$= \quad \$2,000 \text{ x } .655 \quad \longleftarrow \quad 65\frac{1}{2}\% = .655$$
$$= \quad \$1,310.00$$

The cost of the bonds is $1,310.00.

$$\boxed{\text{Interest}} = \boxed{\text{Face Value}} \quad \text{x} \quad \boxed{\text{Annual Rate}}$$

$$= \quad \$2,000 \text{ x } .045 \quad \longleftarrow \quad 4\frac{1}{2}\% = .045$$
$$= \quad \$90.00$$

Leon received $90.00 in interest.

A Find the cost of each bond.

1. Face value: $2,000
   Price: $62\frac{1}{4}$%

   _____

2. Face value: $1,000
   Price: $83\frac{1}{2}$%

   _____

3. Face value: $4,500
   Price: 60%

   _____

4. Face value: $10,000
   Price: $75\frac{1}{4}$%

   _____

B Find the annual interest on each bond.

5. Face value: $4,000
   Interest rate: 5%

   _____

6. Face value: $2,000
   Interest rate: $6\frac{1}{2}$%

   _____

7. Face value: $5,000
   Interest rate: 7%

   _____

8. Face value: $3,000
   Interest rate: $7\frac{1}{4}$%

   _____

C Find the cost and the annual interest paid on each bond.

	Face Value	Price	Cost	Annual Rate	Interest
9.	$5,000	48%		4%	
10.	2,000	65%		$5\frac{1}{2}$%	
11.	4,500	40%		$3\frac{1}{2}$%	
12.	1,000	67%		$6\frac{1}{4}$%	
13.	10,000	82%		$7\frac{1}{2}$%	
14.	6,500	60%		6%	
15.	50,000	72%		7%	
16.	2,500	64%		$6\frac{1}{2}$%	
17.	12,500	76%		7%	
18.	3,000	55%		5%	

19. John Harris bought $5,000 worth of bonds at $65\frac{1}{2}$%. They have
    an annual interest rate of 5%. What is the cost of the bonds, and
    what is the annual interest?   _____

20. Emilia Suarez bought $7,500 worth of bonds at $50\frac{1}{4}$%. They have
    an annual interest rate of 6%. What is the cost of the bonds, and
    what is the annual interest?   _____

Savings Bonds

The United States government sells savings bonds. One type of bond is the series EE. These bonds are guaranteed by the government and can be purchased with a face value from $50 to $10,000. The cost of these bonds is 50% of the face value. The *redemption value* of the bond includes the cost plus interest for the time the holder had the bond. To find the value of the bond when it is redeemed, a chart similar to this one is used.

Redemption Value of $50 Series EE Savings Bonds	
After	Redemption Value
6 months	$25.50
1 year	26.40
$1\frac{1}{2}$ years	27.22
2 years	28.14
3 years	30.28
4 years	32.92
5 years	36.12
6 years	39.24
7 years	42.68
8 years	46.46
9 years	50.64

Example: Steven DeVito bought a $500 bond and redeemed it 6 years later. What is the redemption value of the bond? How much interest did Steve earn?

$$\boxed{\text{Cost of Bond}} = \boxed{\text{Face Value}} \quad \text{x} \quad \boxed{50\%}$$

= $500 x .50 ◄— 50% = .50
= $250

$$\boxed{\text{Redemption Value}} = \boxed{\text{Redemption Value of \$50 Bond}} \quad \text{x} \quad \boxed{\text{Number of \$50 in Face Value}}$$

= $39.24 x 10 ◄— 500 ÷ 50 = 10
= $392.40

The redemption value is $392.40.

$$\boxed{\text{Interest}} = \boxed{\text{Redemption Value}} \quad - \quad \boxed{\text{Cost of Bond}}$$

= $392.40 – $250.00
= $142.40

The interest earned is $142.40.

A Find the cost of each bond.

1. $100 _____
2. $250 _____
3. $50 _____
4. $1,000 _____
5. $10,000 _____
6. $5,500 _____

B Find the redemption value of each bond.

7. Face value: $500
   Time held: 4 years

   _____

8. Face value: $1,000
   Time held: 7 years

   _____

9. Face value: $50
   Time held: 5 years

   _____

10. Face value: $5,000
    Time held: 8 years

    _____

C Find the cost, redemption value, and interest on each bond.

	Face Value	Cost of EE Bond	Time Held	Redemption Value of $50 Bond	Redemption Value	Interest
11.	$200		5 years			
12.	100		2 years			
13.	500		7 years			
14.	1,000		9 years			
15.	50		6 years			
16.	10,000		8 years			
17.	5,000		$1\frac{1}{2}$ years			
18.	400		2 years			
19.	800		3 years			
20.	650		4 years			

Rate of Return

People who own stock receive *dividends*. One way to determine if an investment is a good one is to examine the *annual rate of return*. To find this, compare the dividend to the cost of the stock.

Example: Donald Coleman owns 100 shares of stock. He receives an annual dividend of $3.60 per share. What is his total annual dividend? If he paid $45 per share, what is the rate of return?

Total Annual Dividend	=	No. of Shares	x	Dividend per Share

$$= 100 \times \$3.60$$
$$= \$360.00$$

The total annual dividend is $360.00.

Rate of Return	=	Dividend per Share	÷	Cost per Share

$$= \$3.60 \div \$45.00$$
$$= \$.08 = 8\%$$

The annual rate of return is 8%.

A Find the total annual dividend for each investor.

1. Robert Ochs
   Number of shares: 200
   Dividend per share: $3.25

   _____

2. Lauren Taylor
   Number of shares: 1,000
   Dividend per share: $6.95

   _____

B Find the annual rate of return.

3. T. H. Enterprises
   Cost per share: $18.25
   Annual dividend: $1.46

   _____

4. XY Corporation
   Cost per share: $24.50
   Annual dividend: $2.94

   _____

C Find the total annual dividend and the rate of return.

	Name of Stock	Cost per Share	Number of Shares	Dividend per Share	Total Annual Dividend	Rate of Return
5.	T. C. Corp	$14.50	100	$1.16		
6.	G. E.	36.25	200	2.90		
7.	Amtrax	64.50	50	3.87		
8.	T. B. Tech	28.40	150	1.42		
9.	Val Cox	30.00	80	2.25		
10.	B. C. Foods	42.50	300	5.10		
11.	GMC	44.20	450	2.21		
12.	FT Corp	125.00	1,000	12.50		
13.	ATM	85.50	600	6.84		
14.	H. B. J.	65.00	180	3.90		
15.	Ortex	72.00	250	5.35		

People who own bonds receive *interest.* To determine the rate of return, compare the interest to the cost of the bond.

Example: Donald also has bonds with a face value of $5,000 at a cost of 60%. He receives interest at an annual rate of 6%. What is the annual interest? What is his rate of return?

Cost of Bond	=	Face Value	x	Percent of Face (Price)

= $5,000 x .60 ◄— 60% = .60
= $3,000.00

Annual Interest	=	Face Value	x	Annual Rate

= $5,000 x .06 ◄— 6% = .06
= $300.00

| Rate of Return | = | Annual Interest | ÷ | Cost |

$$= \$300 \div \$3,000$$
$$= .10 = 10\%$$

The rate of return is 10%.

D Find the cost, interest, and rate of return of each bond.

	Face Value	Price	Cost	Annual Rate	Interest	Rate of Return
16.	$4,000	60%		3%		
17.	3,000	80%		8%		
18.	5,000	72%		9%		
19.	40,000	50%		4%		
20.	2,500	75%		6%		
21.	10,000	70%		7%		
22.	6,500	80%		10%		
23.	12,000	50%		6%		
24.	9,500	64%		8%		

25. Nicky bought a $10,000 bond for 64%. It pays an annual interest rate of 8%. What is the rate of return? _____

End-of-Book Test

Understanding Terms

A Write *True* or *False* next to each statement.

_____ 1. The base price of a car represents the total purchase price of the car.

_____ 2. When buying a house, most people pay part of the purchase price in the form of a down payment.

_____ 3. Sales tax is the percentage a person pays on a mortgage loan.

_____ 4. Certificates of deposit usually have a lower interest rate than a savings account.

_____ 5. Owning stock means you own a part of the company that issued the stock.

_____ 6. Savings bonds are sold by the United States government.

_____ 7. Companies that offer credit cards or loans charge interest for the privilege of using their money.

_____ 8. Gasoline, tires, and repairs are examples of variable expenses.

_____ 9. A person earning overtime pay receives less money per hour than a person earning straight-time pay.

_____ 10. A passbook is a record of a person's savings account plus any loans.

Sales Tax

B Calculate the sales tax and the total cost for each item.

	Item Purchased	Selling Price	Tax Rate	Sales Tax	Total Cost
11.	Clock	$62.50	6%		
12.	Milk	2.09	7.5%		
13.	Tires	380.00	7%		
14.	Stationery	12.95	8%		
15.	Scarf	25.00	6.5%		

Fractions

 Add or subtract the following fractions. Write the answers in lowest terms.

16. $\dfrac{2}{3} + \dfrac{3}{4} =$

17. $\dfrac{1}{5} + \dfrac{3}{10} =$

18. $\dfrac{1}{6} + \dfrac{7}{12} =$

19. $\dfrac{1}{2} - \dfrac{1}{3} =$

20. $\dfrac{3}{4} - \dfrac{1}{2} =$

21. $\dfrac{7}{8} - \dfrac{3}{4} =$

Buying a Car

 Calculate the cost of each car.

22. Spencer James bought a new car with a sticker price of $22,500. He made a down payment of 15% and 36 payments of $545.20. How much did the car cost? _____

23. Debbie Bonner traded in her car for a new one. The new car cost $21,450. She received $3,500 for her trade-in. She made 48 payments of $396.40. How much did the car cost? _____

Buying and Selling Stock

E Calculate the cost or profits of the stock transactions.

24. Henry Gonzalez bought 200 shares of stock at $50\frac{1}{2}$. The stockbroker's commission was $59.75. What was the total cost of the stock? _____

25. Amy Lin paid $26\frac{1}{2}$ per share for 300 shares of stock. The commission was $42.50. Two years later she sold the stock for $31\frac{1}{2}$ per share and paid a commission of $50.35. How much profit did she make? _____

Percents

 Write a percent for each fraction.

26. $\dfrac{7}{20} =$

27. $\dfrac{4}{5} =$

28. $\dfrac{11}{20} =$

29. $\dfrac{19}{20} =$

30. $\dfrac{3}{5} =$